South Texas Heroes

A CELEBRATION OF OUR MILITARY

Published by the

Corpus Christi Caller Times

An E.W. Scripps Company

Caller.com

National Archives

U.S. Marines raise the flag on Mount Suribachi on Iwo Jima on Feb. 23, 1945, in Joe Rosenthal's famous photo for the Associated Press.

Table of Contents

INTRODUCTION

"Time will not dim the glory of their deeds."
— Gen. John J. Pershing

One by one they came to our lobby — people bearing photos and keepsakes, answering our call for contributions for our newest book project. The former busboy who became a paratrooper; the young lady from Rockport who wanted her grandpa in our book; the mother of the young man currently serving in Iraq; the woman who served in Algiers; the woman who remembers her father going AWOL while stationed in Hawaii because he had to get home to his family in Corpus Christi before the hurricane hit here — as they came to the lobby, and we heard their stories, our book project was transformed from "our" book to "their" book.

Contributors were endearing, charming, witty and had maintained their sense of humor despite hardships many of us will never experience. One man could no longer write, suffering from immense pain of arthritis. But his story was so compelling that we called for an employee to sit with him in the lobby to write down his information.

To all contributors, we wish to extend our profound thanks for sharing your memories, your photographs and your keepsakes. You honored us by opening your photo albums. But the greatest honor was that you opened your hearts and shared your lives with us. It was that honor that kept us going late at night when we searched through photos and information. It became more than a "labor of love" — it became a "labor of honor" dedicated to military personnel, their families, their friends and all of their stories.

You are all heroes, and you are our heroes — South Texas Heroes.

— *Linda Barajas Montoya,*
project manager

The World Wars

World War II Timeline

Hitler

1933 — 1934

Germany is prostrate under the weight
of reparation penalities imposed on it
by the victors of World War I and the
Versailles Treaty.

ADOLF HITLER becomes chancellor of
Germany's National Coalition Government and dictator.

Hitler becomes Führer and orders the creation of an air force and expansion of
the army and navy.

Militaristic Japanese forces expand on
their invasion of China and Manchuria.

1935 — 1938

Italian dictator BENITO MUSSOLINI,
invades Ethiopia.

The Nuremberg Laws are passed to
prosecute German Jews.

The Nazis abandon the Versailles Treaty.

The swastika is adopted as the official
German emblem and flag.

Neutrality Acts are passed in the United
States.

Mussolini

1939

England signs a treaty promising
to protect Poland.

Germany invades Poland on Sept. 1.
England and France declare war two
days later, and World War II begins.

1940

Germany invades Norway, Denmark,
France, Holland, Belgium
and Luxembourg.

WINSTON CHURCHILL becomes
British prime minister.

Germany, Japan and Italy sign the
Tripartite Pact, creating the Axis
Powers. Hungary, Bulgaria and
Romania later join the alliance.

The Luftwaffe — the German air force
— attacks London. The Blitz begins.

British troops are evacuated
from Dunkirk.

The British win the Battle of Britain,
forcing Hitler to suspend Operation
Sea Lion, the German invasion
of England.

Churchill

1941

The Lend-Lease Bill passes, enabling
Roosevelt to provide aid to the Allies.

The Afrika Korps, led by **Field Marshal
ERWIN ROMMEL,** launches a new
campaign in North Africa.

Germany launches Operation Barbarossa,
the invasion of the Soviet Union.

Rommel

Roosevelt

Nazi Einsatzgruppen begins mass murder
operations.

Churchill and **U.S. President
FRANKLIN D. ROOSEVELT** sign
the Atlantic Charter, outlining the
Anglo-American reasons for war.

German Jews required to wear yellow
stars on clothes.

Operation Typhoon, the German attack on
Moscow, fails.

The Japanese bomb Pearl Harbor, a U.S.
naval base in Hawaii, and also attack
the Philippines, Wake Island, Guam,
Malaya, Thailand, Shanghai and
Midway. Roosevelt vows to win an
"absolute victory" over America's ene-
mies.

The U.S. and England declare war on
Japan, Germany and Italy.

The Japanese invade the Philippines.

Gen. DOUGLAS MacARTHUR moves
his forces to the Bataan Peninsula.

MacArthur

1942

Manila falls to the Japanese.

The Japanese attack MacArthur's forces
in Bataan.

German officials, led by SS Gen. Rein-
hard Heydrich, meet at Wannsee to discuss and launch the "final solution" to
the "Jewish Question."

The first waves of U.S. forces arrive in
England.

Lt. Edward O'Hare of the USS Lexington
becomes the first ace of the war in air
battles near Rabaul.

MacArthur is evacuated from Bataan.
Roosevelt appoints him commander of
the Southwest Pacific Theater.

The Roosevelt administration creates the
War Relocation Authority, which will
send 120,000 Japanese-Americans to
relocation camps.

Admiral CHESTER NIMITZ is named
the commander of the U.S. Pacific
Theater.

U.S. troops on Bataan surrender
to the Japanese. It is the largest army
in American history to surrender.

The Bataan Death March begins: More
than 75,000 Allied troops march 60
miles with no food or water to
Japanese POW camps. More than
5,000 Americans die.

The Battle of Midway is a decisive
victory for the U.S.

**Gen. BERNARD LAW
MONTGOMERY** takes field
command in North Africa.

The Battle of Stalingrad, one of the war's
biggest, most savage and most important

Nimitz

Montgomery

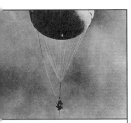

Japanese balloon

senhower

mamoto

alin

Marshall

battles, begins.

The Japanese drop **incendiary bombs from balloons** on Oregon forests, the first time mainland U.S. is bombed.

The carrier Hornet is sunk in the Battle of Santa Cruz off the coast of Guadalcanal.

Operation Torch, the U.S. invasion of North Africa, begins. The operation features the debut of a new field commander, **Lt. Gen. DWIGHT D. EISENHOWER**.

The Japanese retreat from Guadalcanal. Five months of naval and land warfare is over, resulting in an Allied victory.

1943

Allies win battle for Buna, New Guinea.

Churchill and Roosevelt meet in Casablanca.

The Soviets win the battle of Stalingrad, Germany's first major defeat and a turning point in the war for Eastern Europe.

U.S. and German armored forces clash at Kasserine Pass in North Africa.

The USS Lexington, CV-16, formerly the USS Cabot, is commissioned.

Japanese **Adm. ISOROKU YAMAMOTO**, a principal architect of Japanese naval operations, is shot down near Bougainville in the Solomon Islands.

Jewish resistance in the Warsaw ghetto is wiped out. All Jewish ghettos in Poland are soon liquidated.

Allies invade Sicily and then mainland Italy. Mussolini resigns and is arrested.

Italy surrenders to the Allied Powers. Four days later, the Nazis rescue the Italian dictator. As Mussolini rebuilds a fascist regime, the Italian government declares war on Germany.

Tarawa falls to U.S. forces.

Churchill, Roosevelt, and Soviet dictator **JOSEPH STALIN** meet at Teheran.

Roosevelt and **U.S. Army Chief of Staff Gen. GEORGE C. MARSHALL** name Gen. Eisenhower supreme commander of the Allied expeditionary force in Europe.

1944

The Marshall Islands fall to U.S. forces.

U.S. forces attack the Mariana Islands.

Rome falls to the Allies.

Operation Overlord, the Allied invasion of France, begins.

The "Marianas Turkey Shoot" — U.S. fighters shoot down more than 200 Japanese planes. Only 20 U.S. planes are lost.

Marines land on Guam and Tinian in the Marianas.

Assassination attempt on Hitler fails.

Paris is liberated. Allied troops parade through the city. Gen. Eisenhower

Truman

Patton

believes the war will be over by Christmas.

Operation Market-Garden, the Allied invasion of the Netherlands, begins. German resistance is underestimated, and it fails.

U.S. forces under Gen. MacArthur land on Leyte in the southern Philippines. The Battle of Leyte Gulf is a U.S. victory. But the battle sees the first use of a new Japanese tactic: the kamikaze attack.

Roosevelt is re-elected to a fourth term as president. His new vice president is **HARRY S. TRUMAN**.

Germans launch the Ardennes Offensive, also known as the Battle of the Bulge. The battle is the bloodiest ever fought by Americans.

Bastogne is held by the 101st Airborne Division, and the city becomes a symbol of hope for the Allies. Hitler personally orders the city to be taken, and Bastogne is attacked night and day by German armored units.

Lt. Gen. GEORGE S. PATTON, commander of the U.S. Third Army, vows to break through to Bastogne the day after Christmas and does. The German counteroffensive is pushed back.

1945

U.S. troops invade Iwo Jima.

Roosevelt, Churchill and Stalin meet at Yalta.

U.S. forces cross into Germany.

U.S. troops invade Okinawa, one of the war's bloodiest battles.

Roosevelt dies of a cerebral hemorrhage. Harry Truman becomes president.

Soviets launch a final offensive on Berlin.

Mussolini is assassinated.

Hitler kills himself.

Germany surrenders to the Allies on May 8, Truman's 61st birthday.

Operation Downfall, the invasion of Japan, is approved. Gen. MacArthur and Adm. Nimitz will command it.

Truman meets with Stalin, Churchill and new British Prime Minister Clement Attlee in Potsdam. It is the last Big Three meeting.

Atom bombs are dropped on Hiroshima and Nagasaki.

Japan formally surrenders on Sept. 2 to Gen. MacArthur, who will occupy the nation. World War II is over.

The United Nations is born.

Sources:
"A World at Arms: A Global History of World War II," by Gerhard L. Weinberg; The WWII Internet Museum; PBS.org; BBC.com; Texas Parks & Wildlife; Naval Historical Institute; Caller-Times archives

Men read a *Caller-Times* Extra reporting the Japanese attack on Pearl Harbor early Sunday morning.

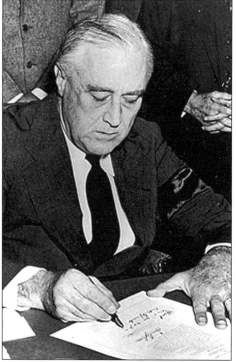

President Roosevelt signs the declaration of war on Japan on Dec. 8, 1941.

Franklin D. Roosevelt asks Congress for a declaration of war against the Empire of Japan

Yesterday, December 7, 1941 — a date which will live in infamy — the United States of America was suddenly and deliberately attacked by naval and air forces of the Empire of Japan.

The United States was at peace with that nation and, at the solicitation of Japan, was still in conversation with its Government and its Emperor looking toward the maintenance of peace in the Pacific. Indeed, one hour after Japanese air squadrons had commenced bombing in Oahu, the Japanese Ambassador to the United States and his colleague delivered to the Secretary of State a formal reply to a recent American message. While this reply stated that it seemed useless to continue the existing diplomatic negotiations, it contained no threat or hint of war or armed attack.

It will be recorded that the distance of Hawaii from Japan makes it obvious that the attack was deliberately planned many days or even weeks ago. During the intervening time the Japanese Government has deliberately sought to deceive the United States by false statements and expressions of hope for continued peace.

The attack yesterday on the Hawaiian Islands has caused severe damage to American naval and military forces. Very many American lives have been lost. In addition American ships have been reported torpedoed on the high seas between San Francisco and Honolulu.

Yesterday the Japanese Government also launched an attack against Malaya. Last night Japanese forces attacked Hong Kong. Last night Japanese forces attacked Guam. Last night Japanese forces attacked the Philippine Islands. Last night the Japanese attacked Wake Island. This morning the Japanese attacked Midway Island.

Japan has, therefore, undertaken a surprise offensive extending throughout the Pacific area. The facts of yesterday speak for themselves. The people of the United States have already formed their opinions and well understand the implications to the very life and safety of our nation.

As Commander-in-Chief of the Army and Navy, I have directed that all measures be taken for our defense.

Always will we remember the character of the onslaught against us. No matter how long it may take us to overcome this premeditated invasion, the American people in their righteous might will win through to absolute victory.

I believe I interpret the will of the Congress and of the people when I assert that we will not only defend ourselves to the uttermost but will make very certain that this form of treachery shall never endanger us again.

Hostilities exist. There is no blinking at the fact that our people, our territory and our interests are in grave danger. With confidence in our armed forces — with the unbounded determination of our people —we will gain the inevitable triumph — so help us God.

I ask that the Congress declare that since the unprovoked and dastardly attack by Japan on Sunday, December seventh, a state of war has existed between the United States and the Japanese Empire.

Source: Franklin D. Roosevelt Presidential Library and Museum

Traffic Toll
DEAD
Nueces County 23
Corpus Christi 4
INJURED
Nueces County 188
Corpus Christi 166
ACCIDENTS INVESTIGATED
Nueces County 1,979

Corpus Christi Caller

The Weather
Cloudy; Sailing Weather Favorable

ESTABLISHED 1883—VOL. 50—NO. 185 — CORPUS CHRISTI, TEXAS, MONDAY MORNING, DECEMBER 8, 1941 — Ten Pages Today—PRICE FIVE CENTS

Japan Goes to War With U. S. in Air Attacks on American Pacific Outposts

Roosevelt To Address Congress

Joint Session Of Legislators Is Scheduled

Speaker Rayburn Says He 'Doesn't Know' If War Will Be Declared

WASHINGTON, Dec. 7. (AP) Senator Connally (D-Texas) announced from the White House steps tonight that President Roosevelt would address a joint session of Congress at 12:30 p. m. tomorrow.

Emerging from the front door of the White House as a meeting of the President's cabinet ended, the chairman of the Senate foreign relations committee said:

"The President will address a joint session of Congress at 12:30 p. m. tomorrow. That is all I can say."

As he made the statement to newspapermen, Secretary of War Stimson left the White House and Senator Hiram Johnson (R-Calif) departed a moment later.

Cabinet members and congressional leaders had met with Mr. Roosevelt to discuss the ominous implications of Japan's declaration of war upon the United States and Great Britain.

Speaker Rayburn said that the President did not tell the conference what he was going to say in tomorrow's message. And when he was asked whether the Chief Executive would propose a declaration of war he replied solemnly:

"I don't know."

Rayburn said that the Chief Executive, cabinet and congressional leaders went over the entire situation and that the President had remarked that some rumors were going about which were unconfirmed.

What these rumors were, the Speaker did not say. A declaration of war, Rayburn asserted, would be one thing on which there would be congressional unity.

Asked whether there had been discussion of discarding politics during the present crisis, House Republican Leader Martin remarked:

"This is a serious moment. We were not talking about politics. Of course there will be more."

The Senate Republican leader, McNary of Oregon, declined to speculate whether the President would request a declaration of war but told reporters:

"The Republicans will all go along with what is done, in my opinion."

Coast Guardsmen Await Navy Orders At Port Aransas

Organization Equipped With Seven Boats for Harbor, Coastal Patrol

Caller-Times News Service

PORT ARANSAS—Capt. James A. Alsup and 30 U. S. Coast Guardsmen stationed here under his command were awaiting orders from the Navy Department tonight as to how they would proceed in new military duties which may be brought on by the fast-developing crisis in the Pacific.

The Coast Guard Station here is equipped with seven boats for harbor and coastal patrol. Some beach patrol work is carried out by trucks.

Exact military duties of the Coast Guardsmen remains confidential, but they are prepared to keep sharp watch on a long section of Texas coast.

Wake Island Said Taken by Japanese

London Hears United States' Possessions Already Occupied

LONDON, Monday, Dec. 8. (AP)—A Reuters dispatch from Shanghai today quoted an unconfirmed report circulated there saying United States owned Wake Island had been occupied by the Japanese.

The British news agency said the Shanghai rumors had it that

Canada To Fight Japanese

OTTAWA, Dec. 7. (UP)—Canada came quickly to the support of the United States tonight with an announcement that a state of war exists between the Dominion and Japan.

The action, taken at an emergency session of the Cabinet, was the first such move by a member of the British Commonwealth of Nations.

Prime Minister W. L. MacKenzie King called the cabinet into session after receiving reports of the Japanese attack upon Hawaii.

A general order was issued to "engage the enemy wherever they may be found."

The order-in-council declaring war on Japan was transmitted by cable to His Majesty the King for his personal signature on behalf of the people of Canada.

The state of war was effective, however, from the moment of announcement here.

Japanese Carrier Said Sunk

NEW YORK, Dec. 7. (UP)—Roundabout, unconfirmed reports from Panama and London said tonight that a Japanese aircraft carrier from which planes operated to attack Pearl Harbor had been sunk by United States Navy ships.

These circulated in Panama and were broadcast from London by CBS Commentator Bob Trout as having been heard there. Trout also said unofficial news bulletins in London announced the sinking of two British cruisers at Singapore.

Mexico Condemns Jap Attack

MEXICO CITY, Dec. 7. (UP)—Foreign Minister Ezequiel Padilla tonight in a signed statement condemned Japan's "aggression" against the United States and re-pledged Mexico's full assistance to her neighboring nation under the Havana Treaty.

Simultaneously the pro-administration newspaper La Prensa of Mexico City demanded that Mexico declare war against Japan—an eventuality which a foreign office source told the United Press was "not impossible."

Padilla dictated his statement by telephone from the resort of Cuernavaca to his private secretary, Jose Valadez, at the foreign office, after consulting President Manuel Avila Camacho at the latter's ranch home there.

Both the President and Padilla cut their week-ends short and were rushing back to the capital tonight.

U.S. Proposed Concessions To Preserve Peace

Hull Denounces Japanese Attack as 'Treacherous'

WASHINGTON, Dec. 7. (AP)—Secretary of State Hull tonight denounced the Japanese attack upon the United States as "treacherous and utterly unprovoked," and made public for the country's information the proposals made to Japan for a peaceful settlement of all Pacific problems and Tokyo's reply.

The usually soft-spoken Tennessean issued a statement in connection with the publication of the document declaring it now was apparent that the Japanese professions of a desire for peace in the conversations held with him by the Japanese envoys had been "infamously false and fraudulent."

Hull Offered Concessions

The Japanese broke off the discussions with the charge that "the attitude of the American government had made it impossible to reach an agreement through further negotiations."

The American note, handed to the Japanese envoys by Hull November 26, called for Tokyo to abandon aggression and offered economic concessions from this country. In reply the Japanese charged that the United States sought to "conspire with Great Britain and other countries to thwart Japan's new order in East Asia."

The salient points of the American note were these:

Japanese withdrawal of all military forces from China and Indo-China.

Agreement by the United States and Japan to recognize only the National Government of China, which now has its temporary capital at Chungking.

U. S. Would Cede Rights

The United States and Japan to give up all extraterritorial rights in China and seek to induce Great Britain and other nations to give up theirs.

Negotiations to be undertaken between the United States and Japan for a trade agreement based upon reciprocal most-favored nation treatment and reduction of trade barriers by both countries, including an undertaking by the United States to bind raw silk on the free list.

The removal of freezing restrictions on Japanese funds here and on American funds in Japan.

Agreement on a plan for stabilization of the dollar-yen rate.

An agreement that no pact which either country has concluded with any third power shall be interpreted to conflict with the fundamental purpose of the proposed agreement—the establishment and preservation of peace throughout the Pacific.

(That stipulation was interpreted here as binding Japan to renounce her ties with Germany and Italy.)

Sought Non-Aggression Pact

The United States and Japan would endeavor to conclude a non-aggression pact among the British Empire, China, Japan, The Netherlands, the Soviet Union, Thailand and the United States.

All of the governments signing that non-aggression pact would join in guaranteeing the territorial integrity of French Indo-China.

Hull disclosed that a Japanese plan had been communicated to the State Department June 21 but

(Turn to Page 2, Column 2)

FDR Told Of More Bombing

WASHINGTON, Dec. 7. (AP) The White House announced tonight that during President Roosevelt's conference with legislative leaders and members of the cabinet he received word from Gen. Douglas MacArthur the "enemy planes were over Central Luzon in the Philippines about 8 p. m., Eastern standard time; that a bombing attack has been made on Davoa at the southern end of the southern Island of Mindanoa, and that another attack has been made on Camp John Hayes at Baguio in the northern mountains of Luzon."

The White House announcement said that "so far no essential damage had been reported."

Legislators at Meeting

The announcement, which also reported the decision of the President to address Congress at 12:30 p. m., Eastern Standard Time, tomorrow, said,

"At 8:30 p. m., the cabinet met with the President in the White House. Shortly after nine legislative leaders from both branches of the Congress, and both parties, arrived and participated in a joint meeting with the President and the Cabinet:

"The President reviewed for them all information received up to that time and gave them also other information not yet verified and which at the time had to be classified as rumor. The President told them of doubtless very heavy losses sustained by the Navy and also large losses sustained by the Army in the island of Hu.

Message Not Written

"The legislative leaders approved the request of the President to address a joint session of the House and Senate on Monday at 12:30 p. m., Eastern Standard time. It should be emphasized that the mesage to the Congress has not yet been written and its tenor will of course, depend on further information received between 11 o'clock tonight and noon tomorrow. Further news is coming in all the time.

"During the conference the President received a report from General MacArthur that enemy planes were over central Luzon in the Philippines about 8 p. m. Washington time; that a bombing attack has been made on Davoa at the southern end of the southern island of Mindanoa, and that another atack has been made on Camp John Hayes at Baguio in the northern mountains of Luzon. So far no essential damage had been reported."

Navy To Escort All 'Important Vessels,' Commandant Says

BREMERTON, Wash., Dec. 7. (AP)—Rear Admiral Charles S. Freeman, 13th Naval District commandant, announced today the Navy would provide armed escorts for "all important vessels from northwest and Alaska ports," in view of the Japanese attack.

ATTACKED BY JAPANESE—The United States Battleship Oklahoma, shown here, was reported yesterday to have been set afire by Japanese air raiders in the attack on Pearl Harbor at Honolulu. Two other unnamed craft in the harbor also were reported attacked.

Japanese Attack Called 'Treachery' By Capt. Bernhard

Naval Air Station Will Launch Wartime Schedule Today: All Leaves Are Cancelled And More Guards Posted as Emergency Move

"Treachery" was the label with which Captain Alva D. Bernhard, commanding officer of Corpus Christi's Naval Air Station, branded the attack of Japan on Pearl Harbor and other American possessions in the Pacific early Sunday.

"There is indignation among the Navy men of the station. The Japanese government performed an act of treachery even as peaceful negotiations were in progress," Captain Bernhard said.

The station has been virtually on a wartime footing all along, but Captain Bernhard announced cancellation of all leaves of officers and enlisted men effective Monday morning. His order included additional guards being placed about the station and a general "tightening down" has gone into effect. Persons without identification tags will no longer be permitted to enter.

"We'll go on turning out pilots for the Navy," the captain, veteran of 36 years in the air and on the seas, commented. "That's our job."

From the station, soon to reach peak performance, pilots will roll off the "assembly lines" at the rate of about 3,600 a year. Already Navy pilots ready for duty with the fleet are being graduated at the rate of about one a day.

Started on the bleak sands of Flour Bluff Point in June, 1940, the station already has reached peak intake of 300 cadets a month.

"Certainly we are upset," Captain Bernhard said. "We are all upset. My cook, Rosales, is upset. Not long ago he was on the U. S. S. Oklahoma which the Japanese set afire in Pearl Harbor Sunday. Rosales knew a lot of the fellows on the Oklahoma."

The captain, realistic Navy man that he is, expressed sorrow that the Japanese had seen fit to attack the United States.

"I'm glad Japan struck the first blow," he said, "even though it was not expected so soon. War in the Pacific has been inevitable for years, and everybody in the Army and Navy knew it."

He declared that the indignation among the men at the station here flared as a result of the "treachery of the Japanese war act."

"That bombing had been planned for months," he said. "It was no trumped up affair. Bombing operations aren't worked up suddenly on Sunday morning. They

(Turn to Page 2, Column 3)

Outgoing Messages Will Be Censored

Both Navy and War Departments Make Announcements

WASHINGTON, Dec. 7. (AP)—The Navy Department announced tonight that a censorship had been placed on all outgoing cablegrams and radio messages from the United States and its outlying possessions.

No other information was disclosed about the censorship. The three-line announcement said:

"The Navy Department announced tonight that censorship on all outgoing cablegrams and radio messages from the United States and its outlying possessions had been placed in effect."

Shortly before, the War Department had issued this memorandum to the press:

"All information relative to strength, location, designation, location and movement of U. S. troops or Army transports outside the continental limits of the United States are designated by the War Department as secret and will be so considered under the law."

Presumably the reference to "the law" meant that any violators would be subject to the punitive provisions of the espionage act.

(At New York The Associated Press was advised by communications agencies that the Navy had invoked a censorship on Manila and Honolulu, prohibiting messages "outbound" from both Pacific points).

Official Says Draft Age May Be Cut

State Officer Predicts 18-Year-Old Boys Will Be Called

FORT WORTH, Dec. 7. (AP)—Adjt. Gen. J. Watt Page, state director of Selective Service, on learning that hostilities with Japan had broken out, predicted that the minimum age of selectees would be lowered from 21 to 18.

"It is a matter for Congress to determine, of course," General Page said, "but it seems to me that this will have to be done and that in all probability it also will be necessary to raise the age limit back to 36. Many of the boards throughout the nation have just about exhausted

Nye Says Jap War Caused By British

PITTSBURGH, Dec. 7. (UP)—Sen. Gerald P. Nye, R., N. D., said here tonight that the Japanese attack on the United States naval base at Pearl Harbor was "just what Britain had planned for us."

After speaking at an America First rally here, the isolationist leader told reporters:

Cadet Reaction to Japanese Attack on U. S. Possessions Runs From Joy to Grave Concern

By LOUIS ANDERSON

Japan just shouldn't oughta.

That's the general opinion of Naval Air Station cadets and enlisted men, based on an unofficial poll last night.

Comments ranged from happiness over a Japanese war declaration, to depression from one who said he "didn't hate nobody."

A chief machinist's mate who spent three years in the Orient and only recently returned, said: "We should get going immediately. I believe we could knock the Japs out in two months. What I can't figure is how they managed to get through our patrols at Pearl Harbor. When I was there we had a strong protective line."

A cadet in the pool said it was "a relief" to have war declared because it "would step up lessons at the base."

A cadet: "It's just too bad we didn't [illegible] the Japs have plenty of guts to declare war even under Nazi pressure."

Enlisted man in the ship service: "I was thinking about asking for a transfer to Hawaii, but not now."

Marine: "It's no surprise to me. I spent a year in the Far East and three of my buddies are there now. I guess I won't be hearing from them."

Cadet: "I was sitting on the divan with my girl when I heard the war declaration over the radio. I was too stunned then, as my mouth dropped to my knees, but I'm more mentally prepared for it now."

Cadet: "It's a good thing this war—it will warm us up for the big one to come."

A mild-mannered chief [illegible] man, asked his opinion, smiled [illegible] and admitted he knew the war was coming but the shock was in the reality of its [illegible] married and transferred three times by the Navy in the past six weeks, said he had left Pearl Harbor several weeks ago, but the move "was a surprise."

A woman civil service employee said she expected the war eventually, but "I hate it because I know what effect it will have on these cadets here."

Another cadet, college graduate in economics and politics, said, "It's the handwriting on the wall. My study told me war would occur in the Pacific before the Atlantic way back in 1939. The war was inevitable."

Two youthful cadets approached, laconically said, "We are ready," but deplored that in the future they would have to wear uniforms in Corpus Christi. "I just ordered me a new suit," one commented without enthusiasm.

In the world's largest Naval air training base, one of the cadets

Honolulu, Pearl Harbor Objects Of Bombing Raids

Britain Also Included in Declaration of Hostilities as Nipponese Forces Move on Malaya; Rain of Bombs Falls on Hawaii

By THE ASSOCIATED PRESS

Japanese warplanes made a deadly assault on Honolulu and Pearl Harbor Sunday in the foremost of a series of surprise attacks against American possessions throughout the Pacific.

Three hours later the Japanese government declared war on the United States and Great Britain.

Soon a second wave of Japanese bombers roared over shocked Honolulu.

The Japanese also bombed Singapore, and the British announced that the Japanese had landed in North Malaya and were being engaged. The Tokyo radio said the British colony of Hongkong also was attacked and that 63 American soldiers had been disarmed at Tientsin, China.

The Japanese aggression, which the United States officially and unequivocally described as treacherous and utterly unprovoked, bore these first fruits for the empire:

Up to 350 U. S. soldiers killed and more than 300 wounded at Hickam Field, Hawaiian Islands;

The U. S. Battleship Oklahoma set afire and two other U. S. ships at Pearl Harbor attacked;

Heavy damage to Honolulu residence districts, where there were unnumbered casualties.

Torpedoing of a lumber-laden U. S. Army transport between Hawaii and San Francisco;

Bombing of the Philippine Islands;

Capture of the U. S. Pacific islet of Wake and bombing of Guam;

Seizure of the International Settlement at Shanghai;

Capture of the U. S. gunboat Wake at Shanghai, and destruction of the British gunboat Peterel nearby.

There was little news of United States defensive actions, except the report that a number of the attacking planes at Honolulu had been shot down in dogfights over the city; an unconfirmed report that a Japanese aircraft carrier had been sunk off Hawaii, and announcement that U. S. Army and Navy forces had started carrying out secret instructions long since issued to them in event of just such an emergency.

A formal U. S. declaration of war could not come until Monday at the earliest, and Britain summoned her Parliament to meet today for similar action. President Roosevelt, the cabinet and congressional leaders met Sunday night.

The Dutch government in London, the Dutch East Indies, Canada, and the little Central American nation of Costa Rica, near the blacked-out Canal Zone, quickly declared war on Japan.

At the exact moment Japan was irrevocably embarking on her course of "conquer or die," her emissaries in Washington were seeking still another appointment to continue peace talks with which they have consumed the time since last August, with every protestation of good faith.

Finally, when they saw Secretary of State Hull and gave him the latest statement of Japan's position, he told them he never had seen a document "so crowded with falsehoods and distortions."

With embarrassed smiles, the Japanese left.

First announcement that the Japanese had attacked Manila in the Philippines appeared premature, but subsequently a pro-Axis radio station in Shanghai declared there had been an attack which caused great damage:

In both Manila and Honolulu, said the Shanghai broadcast, the Japanese used dive-bombers to cause terrific destruction and many deaths.

Germany, officially and gleefully, declared:

"As a result of constantly increasing warmongering of the American President Roosevelt in recent weeks, the first clashes between Japanese and United States armed forces occurred today."

Details of Japan's explosive rupture of the peace of the Pacific came from many sources.

Announcing the President's action for the protection of American territory, Presidential Secretary Stephen Early declared that, so far as is known now the attacks were "made wholly without warning—when both nations were at peace—and were delivered within an hour of the time that the Japanese ambassadors had gone to the State Department to hand to the Secretary of State Japan's reply to the Secretary's memorandum of the 26th.

Promptly, Navy officers said that long prepared counter measures against Japanese surprise attacks had been ordered into operation and were "working smoothly."

There was a disposition in some quarters here to wonder whether the attacks had not been ordered by the Japanese military authorities because they feared the President's direct negotiations with the Emperor might lead to an about-face in Japanese policy and the consequent loss of face by he present ruling factions in Japan.

No official used the word war in reporting any of the developments, but with the series of events there could be no doubt that the Far Eastern situation had at last exploded, that the United States was at war, and that the conflict which began in Europe was spreading over the entire world.

Little information was immediately available regarding the strength of the Japanese air attacks.

Dispatches from Honolulu said, however, that at least

Caller-Times archives

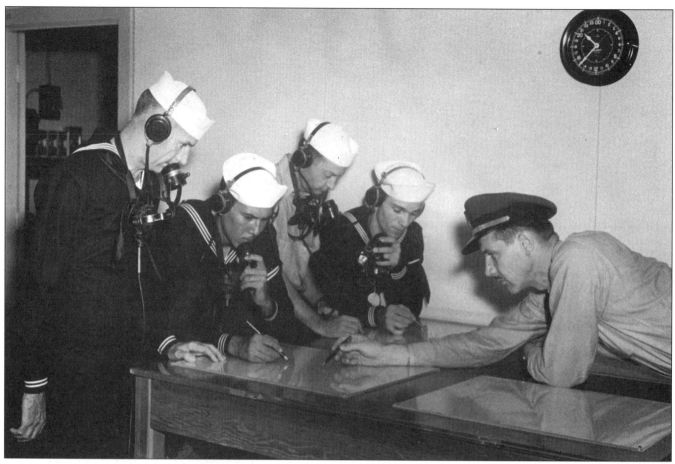

Caller-Times file

Lt. Cmdr. J.W. Sullivan (right) marks a plotting board with a pencil.

Contributed by Mildred Stedman

As the United States mobilized for war in Europe and in the Pacific, memories of the Great War a generation before were still painfully vivid, especially for the survivors of that conflict who now witnessed new shadows of war loom over their friends and family. Army Sgt. Major Robert E. McCullough served in France and Germany from 1918 to 1920. He died in Corpus Christi in August 1978.

Caller-Times file

Edgar S. Malone (center) and Georg Storms (right) at a Army camp in Oklahoma before shipping out to England. The man on the left is unidentified.

Texas Parks & Wildlife

Eleven Army nurses assemble as prisoners of war at a POW camp in the South Pacific during World War II.

Contributed by Annie Lauderdale

Singing into the night

In 1943, Capt. James Roy Lauderdale, a member of the 12th Air Force, was stationed at an air base near Vesuvius, Italy. His missions included dropping British spies into Germany and flying wounded partisans out of Yugoslavia. Landing areas were dry river beds, fields or any flat land. People held lanterns to serve as runway lights. Lauderdale had great respect for the British spies. The spies would parachute into hostile territory with a small folding bicycle, money and the barest of necessities. Lauderdale remembers how the British spies would sing on the plane or as they parachuted into the night.

National A

U.S. dive bombers soar over the burning carcass of a Japanese ship during the Battle of Midway in June 1942. The smoking ship may be the cruiser Mikuma.

The Mikuma, a Japanese heavy cruiser abandoned by its crew, burns as it sinks into the Pacific Ocean at the end of the Battle of Midway on June 6, 1942. Two torpedoes protrude from their portside tubes. U.S. dive bombers from the USS Enterprise sank the cruiser.

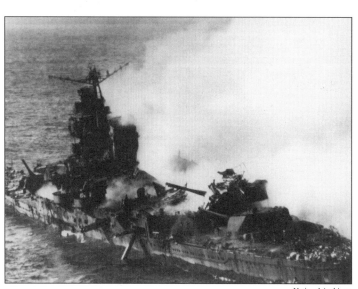

National Archives

National Ar

TBD Devastators of Torpedo Squadron 6 on board USS Enterprise unfold their wings as they prepa take off to participate in the Battle of Midway on 4, 1942. Only four planes in this squadron retu from the day's combat.

National Archives

...nese Nakajima B5N 'Kates' race past the USS Yorktown after launching their torpedoes on June 4, 1942. The carrier is already listing to port from a torpedo strike.

National Archives

...flight deck of the USS Yorktown leans at a perilous angle shortly after an attack by a Japan-...orpedo plane, which made two hits on the aircraft carrier, during the Battle of Midway.

National Archives

Dense smoke billows from the USS Yorktown's funnel after the first Japanese attack on the carrier during the June 1942 Battle of Midway. As damage controlmen deal with the damage, anti-aircraft guns (left) remain on alert for the next attack.

Contributed photo

William B. Miller (back row, third from left) was part of 'Hayward's Hellions,' a Navy squadron that prowled the South Pacific in B-24 Liberator bombers.

Naval Historical Center

The USS Corpus Christi, PF-44, was a Tacoma-class patrol frigate that saw service with the Coast Guard during World War II. It was commissioned on Jan. 29, 1944, and decommissioned on Aug. 2, 1946.

Sgt. Jean White Tanner (holding flag) parades w: other American women in front palace in Algier: 1943. Tanner w: part of a Wome Army Auxiliary Corps unit and served as a secretary on Ge Eisenhower's s:

Contributed by Jean W. Tanner

O. D. Walraven (left), who grew up in Kingsville, flew more than 30 missions as a tail-gunner on B-17's and B-24's in the European Theater. Bill Walraven (middle) was a radarman on a PT boat stationed at Midway Island. He moved to Corpus Christi in 1952. Ferrell Walraven (right) saw action at Guam, the Marianas, the Ryukyus and China, and he took part in the occupation of Japan. He also lived in Corpus Christi.

Contributed by Bill Walraven

Contributed by Dana S. Green

a S. Green (lower right-hand corner), and the Incredible 305th he 'Can Do' Bombers.

Contributed by William Anthony Chapman

U.S. Army Air Forces Lt. Col. William Warren Chapman Jr., part of the 405th Fighter Bomber Group, 509th Squadron, next to his plane in Europe in 1941.

Contributed by Maxine Edmondson Flournc

Maxine Edmondson Flournoy, a member of Women Airforce Service Pilots, prepares for a mission in 1943. The WASPs served in many crucial capacities during World War II, and 38 were killed in the line of duty. When legislation designed to move them into the Army Air Forces failed to pass the Senate, they were disbanded in December 1944. A bill giving 'veteran status to the WASPs passed Congress on March 8, 1979. But their inspirational effect on subsequent generations of women pilots began much sooner and continues today.

Private First Class Julius Marks Rosenberg is a new man after a refreshing shower in New Guinea in May 1943. Rosenberg served with the 593rd Amphibian Engineers.

Contributed photo

Contributed by Vera V. See

Florine V. Mathews (left) sits with Joe Medwick of the Brooklyn Dodgers on April 25, 1943. Medwick autographed the phot

Contributed by Vera V. See

Florine V. Matthews (center) sings with friends in 1943.

Caller-Times file

B-17 tailgunner C.H. Harrel (right, front row) with his crew and their plane in Bassingbourn, England, in December 1943.

Contributed photo

Scott D. Leininger (left) and Charles R. Steffler participated in air attacks on Italy's Mediterranean bases off the African coast in 1944.

Caller-Times file

Joe Kenny (center), pilot of a B-17, and Robert F. Hearn (right), his co-pilot and a native of Rockport, with another crew member at an air base after returning from their mission on D-Day, June 6, 1944. Their B-17 was part of the 8th Air Force, 401st Bomb Group. This bomb group led more than 1,000 bombers from the 8th Air Force in support of the Allied invasion of northern France.

National Archives

Master Sgt. Raymo
A. Muniz sent hom
this portrait for
Christmas in 1943.
Muniz served in th
Air Force from 194
to 1972. He was st
tioned in the South
Pacific, China, Bur
and India.

Contributed by Raymond Muniz

Contributed by Steve and Susie R

Contributed by Willena Quinn

John L. Quinn Jr. was stationed in Riverside, Calif., in the fall of 1943 for training. He was part of an anti-aircraft artillery searchlight battalion and served in the Army from 1943 to 1946.

'90-Day Wonders' was the name given to pilots who trained to fly bomber
Naval Air Station Corpus Christi and received their wings in only 90 da
Among the '90-Day Wonders' was Lt. W. J. 'Wrangler' Roberts (top cent
Roberts served in the Philippines and Japan from 1942 to 1945.

In 1943, Lt. Col. Alex Cox (center) hunted and killed these leopards that were killing people in Assam, India. Cox was honored in China for training elements of the Chinese army.

Contributed by Genevieve Cox

Contributed by Harvey F. Olander

rvey F. Olander next to a German bomber shot down Algiers, Algeria.

Contributed by Yvette Jaurigui Lara

Ramiro D. Garcia of Corpus Christi (top left) relaxes with his Texan friends in April 1944.

Caller-Times

The crew of the USS Lexington, CV-2, abandon ship during the Battle of the Coral Sea in May 1942. Two Japanese torpedoes and three bombs struck the aircraft carrier on May 8. Firestorms swept through the ship but were quickly suppressed. Later, an internal explosion rocked the ship, and the captain orde the carrier abandoned. U.S. warships nearby recovered the crew. A destroyer fi two torpedoes into the Lexington, sending CV-2 to the bottom of the ocean.

Caller-Times file

The USS Lexington, CVS-16, refuels at sea in 1966. The aircraft carrier would serve for 25 more years before being decommissioned and moved to the Corpus Christi bayfront, where it sits today as a museum.

H.G. McPhail (from left), Hap Arnold and Lt. Charles R. Richardson in the ward room of a ship somewhere in the Pacific in 1945. Richardson served in North Africa, the Mediterranean and the South Pacific.

Contributed photo

Lt. J. Patrick McGloin served as a naval aviator from 1942 to 1946.

Contributed by Geraldine D. McGloin

Contributed by Regina Snyder

Obstacle Course, Camp Callan.

Contributed by Tex Villarreal

postcard mailed on April 7, 1943, to Josefa Villarreal in Corpus Christi.

Capt. Wilson P. Snyder, U.S. 3rd Army, 260th Regiment, Company K, among the remains of a town square in Nuremberg, Germany, in 1945. He served in the Army from 1943 to 1946.

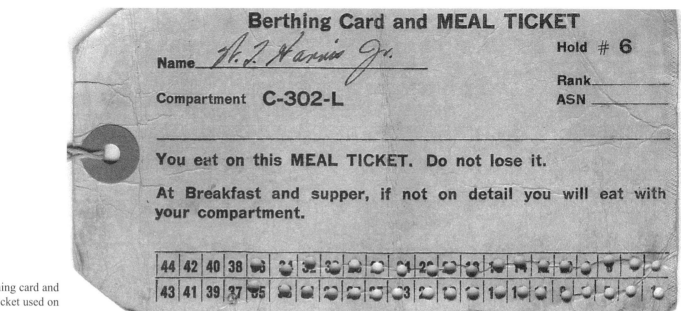

Berthing Card and MEAL TICKET

Name _H. J. Harris Jr._

Hold # 6

Compartment **C-302-L**

Rank _____

ASN _____

You eat on this **MEAL TICKET**. Do not lose it.

At Breakfast and supper, if not on detail you will eat with your compartment.

A berthing card and meal ticket used on a troop ship.

Contributed by Doreen Harris

Contributed photo

Marine Sgt. Overton Randolph Hale served in the South Pacific and at Iwo Jima from 1941 to 1945.

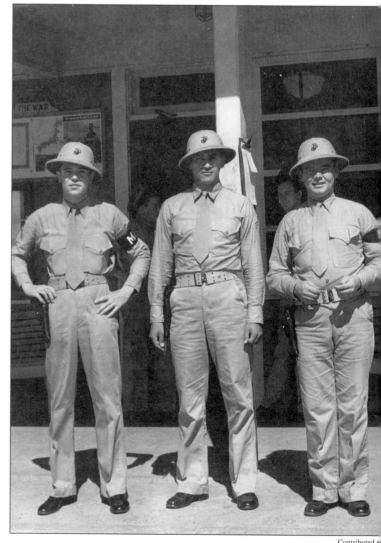

Contributed

William W. Bodine (center) served in the military police at Naval Air Station Corpus Christi in 1945.

EXTRA — Corpus Christi Caller — EXTRA

ESTABLISHED 1883—VOL. 61—NO. 280   CORPUS CHRISTI, TEXAS, TUESDAY MORNING, JUNE 6, 1944   Sixteen Pages Today—PRICE FIVE CENTS

Allies Land in France

Invasion Bulletins

NEW YORK, June 6 (AP)—The London Radio, in a Dutch language broadcast recorded by NBC, warned European underground workers today to report to their leaders with all speed and to "be prepared for anything."

"Keep away from military installations," the broadcast said. Underground members report to your trusted leaders. Act with speed. Be prepared for anything. There is bombardment in the Port of Le Havre."

WASHINGTON, June 6 (AP)—A War Department report from "a front line town" on the coast of England said today that the jumpoff of Allied troops for the invasion of Europe "began in a small way" from that point.

"First, several advance parties of the assault troops marched into the landing stages of this port, clambered aboard the blunt-nosed assault craft and a little later climbed on the larger craft swinging at anchor farther out in the harbor," the report said.

NEW YORK, June 6 (AP)—Gen. Charles De Gaulle has arrived in England, it was announced today in a broadcast from supreme headquarters, Allied Expeditionary Force. NBC monitored the broadcast.

SUPREME HEADQUARTERS, ALLIED EXPEDITIONARY FORCE, June 6 (AP)—It can now be revealed that the Allies have been conducting a series of feints in advance of the invasion today. These feints were predicted several days ago by Prime Minister Churchill, and were designed to fool the Germans so they would never know when the blow was coming.

WASHINGTON, June 6 (AP)—Elmer Davis, director of the office of War Information, today warned the American public that the German radio may be trying to build up a reputation for accuracy in their news reports of the invasion so "they can put one over on the Allies later."

LONDON, June 6 (AP)—The German News Agency DNB said in a broadcast early before the E W T that Anglo-American troops had been enforced at dawn at the mouth of the Seine River in the Le Havre area.

NEW YORK, June 6 (AP)—King Haakon of Norway in an invasion broadcast from London warned his people against premature uprisings, said a broadcast from Supreme Headquarters, Allied Expeditionary Force, heard by NBC. The king broadcast special orders to both organized and unorganized resistance groups in Norway.

LONDON, June 6 (AP)—The sun broke through heavy clouds at times in the Dover Strait area this first day of the Allied invasion of Western Europe. After a daybreak shower there was sunshine, but later banks of heavy clouds swept up from the northwest. There were further sunny periods, although the outlook was less settled. The wind had blown fairly hard during the night, but lost some of its strength after dawn. A moderate sea was running.

NEW YORK, June 6—The Rumanian home radio announced today at 8:07 a. m. Rumanian time, that "enemy formations are over the Belgrade area of Yugoslavia flying northeast toward Rumania," the Federal communications reported.

LONDON, June 6 (AP)—The Berlin Radio said today that "combined British-American landing operations against the western coast of Europe from the sea and air stretching over the entire area between Cherbourg and Le Havre."

WASHINGTON, Tuesday, June 6 (AP)—General of the Armies John J. Pershing, in a statement headed "American Troops Have Landed in Western Europe," said today that he had "every confidence" that the invasion "will win through to victory."

LONDON, Tuesday, June 6 (AP)—Buckingham Palace announced at 10 a. m. (4 a. m. E.W.T.) that King George would broadcast later today.

June 6 (AP)—Headquarters of the European theater of operations reported to the War Department today that Allied aircraft covering the invasion "are hitting any target that has a bearing on the strength of the armies at the front."

Roosevelt Says Collapse of Germany Not Yet in Sight

By HOWARD FLIEGER

WASHINGTON, June 5 (AP)—Hailing the capture of Rome with the jubilant phrase "one up and two to go," President Roosevelt declared tonight that the aim now is to drive Germany "to the point where she will be 'unable to recommence world conquest for a generation hence."

Mr. Roosevelt, in nation-wide radio broadcast, cautioned that this struggle with the Nazis would be tough and costly and that the day of Germany's surrender "lies some distance" ahead.

Whether his reaffirmation that the fight would be pressed until Germany surrenders was a reply to the recent speech of Pope Pius XII was not stated. The Pope asserted last week that the idea that the war must end either in complete victory or complete destruction is a stimulant toward prolonging the conflict and prevent hope for an early peace.

Speaking of Rome as the great symbol of Christianity, the President declared "it will be a source of deep satisfaction that the foundation of the Pope and of Vatican City is assured by the armies of the United States."

But, he declared that no thanks are due Hitler and his generals "if Rome was spared the devastation which the Germans wreaked on Naples and other Italian cities."

"The Allied generals maneuvered so skillfully," he said, "that the Nazis could have stayed long enough to damage Rome at the risk of losing their armies."

"Our victory," Mr. Roosevelt continued, "comes at an excellent time, while our Allied forces are poised for another strike at Western Europe and while armies of other Nazi soldiers nervously await our assault. And our gallant Russian Allies continue to make their power felt more and more."

The President extended to Italy the invitation to help in establishing a lasting peace and said.

"We shall have to pass through a long period of greater effort and fiercer fighting before we get into Germany itself. The Germans have retreated thousands of miles, all the way from the gates of Cairo, through Libya and Tunisia and Sicily and Southern Italy.

"They have suffered serious losses, but not great enough yet to cause their collapse."

In Italy, the President said, the people had lived so long under the corrupt rule of Mussolini that, in spite of the tinsel at the top, their economic condition had grown steadily worse. Our troops have found starvation, malnutrition, disease, a deteriorating educational system and lowered public health —all by-products of the Fascist...

Paratroopers Strike First Invasion Blow

By HOWARD COWAN

WITH UNITED STATES PARACHUTE TROOPS, June 6 (AP)—American paratroopers—mostly battle-hardened veterans of the Sicilian and Italian campaigns—landed behind Hitler's Atlantic Wall today to plant the first blow of the long-awaited western front squarely in the enemy's midst.

Their toughest, wariest men of war executed from faint-assault skies in an awesome operation.

Twin-engined C-47s—sisters of the airborne troop transports C-47s, glinting across the skies, simultaneously towing troop-laden gliders, aloft in a single phenomenal blow paving the way for naval assault forces.

There was no immediate indication that local demands of flashing steel and well-armed but was not succeeding in the execution in plans rehearsed for months in preparation for the liberation of occupied Europe.

Armed with weapons from the most primitive to the most modern, the paratroopers' mission was to disrupt and demoralize the Germans' communications inside the Nazis' own lines.

Invasion News Spreads Quickly

Even though the invasion came at a time when Corpus Christi people usually are asleep, Caller-Times phones began ringing within half a minute after the first Allied "Flash" came over the leased wire.

First call came from the Medical Professional Hospital where the head nurse said her patients had become excited after hearing church bells ringing.

"God be with you" was the comment of an unidentified man who made the second call. He inquired the most polite manner, "Young lady, can you tell me the meaning of the bells," before adding the prayer which was reflected in the words of all other callers.

A few minutes later came the most excited call which the office had received with warning.

"The church bells have begun ringing, and I presumed that it signaled the invasion," she was inquired. "But now they have stopped and I'm calling to see if that means another false alarm."

"That's fine," the inquirer sighed when informed that this...

Eisenhower's Order of Day Reflects Allies' Confidence

SOMEWHERE IN GREAT BRITAIN, Tuesday, June 6 (AP)—Text of the order of the day issued by Gen. Dwight D. Eisenhower to each individual of the Allied Expeditionary Force.

"Soldiers, sailors and airmen of the Allied Expeditionary Force:

"You are about to embark upon the great crusade toward which we have striven these many months. The eyes of the world are upon you. The hopes and prayers of liberty-loving people everywhere march with you. You will bring about the destruction of the German war machine, the elimination of Nazi tyranny over the oppressed peoples of Europe, and security for ourselves in a free world.

"Your task will not be an easy one. Your enemy is well trained, well equipped, and battle-hardened. He will fight savagely.

"But this is the year 1944. Much has happened since the Nazi triumphs of 1940-41."

The United Nations have inflicted upon the Germans great defeat in open battle, man to man. Our air offensive has seriously reduced their strength in the air and their capacity to wage war on the ground.

Our home fronts have given us an overwhelming superiority in weapons and munitions of war, and placed at our disposal great reserves of trained fighting men. The tide has turned.

The free men of the world are marching together to victory. I have full confidence in your courage, devotion to duty and skill in battle. We will accept nothing less than full victory.

Good luck.

And let us all beseech the blessing of Almighty God upon this great and noble undertaking.

Jap Warships Sunk in South Pacific Area

By ROBERT EUNSON

ADVANCED ALLIED HEADQUARTERS, New Guinea, Tuesday, June 6 (AP)—American bombers have extended westward ranging along the foul reported bay of Japanese warships in their lengthy smash, when long-range planes sank one destroyer and left another in sinking condition, headquarters announced today.

These two separate operations highlighted renewed aerial warfare which produced stiff sky battles over the Japanese naval base at Truk in the Caroline Islands and the American-invaded Schouten Islands off the Dutch New Guinea north coast. Seventeen Japanese planes were shot down against the loss of one American bomber in these engagements.

Land's attack on Biak, main Schouten island, remained fluid a consensus of recently-landed reinforcements outflanked the Japanese and approached the Mokmer airdrome, a prime objective, from the north. They were ten miles from the airstrip. Another American column remained about two miles east of Mokmer.

During the night of June 3-4, a small force of Liberator bombers ranged out over the Halmaheras Sea, northeast of Dutch New Guinea sank one Japanese destroyer and left two other "small vessels of Marotai Island.

During the same night Catalina patrol planes, 50 miles off at Manokwari in North Dutch New Guinea, scored two direct hits on a Japanese destroyer, leaving the vessel dead in the water.

Admiralty-based Liberators hammered Truk with 79 tons of bombs Saturday. This marked a continuation of heavy assaults to Southwest Pacific planes, in conjunction with other attacks by bombers from the Central Pacific.

Seven Japanese fighters were shot down Saturday, and one Liberator failed to return.

Yank Planes Bomb Kurile Isles Again

PEARL HARBOR, June 5 (AP)—Army and Navy planes hitting the Kuriles again, attacked enemy installations within 400 miles of the Japanese mainland Sunday and two Central Pacific escort carrier raids send out enemy positions on the island of Truk Atoll in the Carolines last Saturday and Sunday.

Church Bells Call People To Prayer

Shortly before 3 o'clock this morning Corpus Christi Cathedral bells chimed the pre-arranged signal that the Allies had launched the invasion of Europe.

They awakened many of the sleeping population to the realization that the day had come and many prayers and prayers of liberty-loving people everywhere marched with joy. You will bring about the destruction of the German war machine, the elimination of Nazi tyranny over the oppressed peoples of Europe, and security for ourselves in a free world.

With daylight, the doors of all churches will open for prayer services led by their ministers. Many of the business houses here persuaded to stated their intention of closing on D-day, which can now carry the dateline, June 6.

King Victor Steps Aside As Monarch

By SID FEDER

NAPLES, June 5 (AP)—King Victor Emmanuel III stepped aside as monarch of Italy today as the price he had long been willing to pay previously had said he would do once victory had said he would do once the liberation of Rome and handed to his 39-year-old son, Crown Prince Umberto, all "royal prerogatives."

Italian political pressure had been brought to bear against him since the conquest of Naples.

In a decree signed by himself and countersigned by Premier Marshal Pietro Badoglio, head of the Italian Liberation Government, the king named his son lieutenant general of the realm.

The monarch, however, retained his title as head of the House of Savoy and remains as king without power.

King Victor Emmanuel, who became ruler July 29, 1900, had announced last April 12 his "irrevocable" decision to withdraw from public life "on the day on which Allied troops enter Rome," and to turn his powers over to the crown prince.

Prince Umberto opposed Fascism in Italy at the start but later made a truce with Mussolini.

In effect, Umberto becomes the king's regent.

The withdrawal was presented to the council of ministers this morning, an announcement by the ministry of the interior said tonight. The decree, signed by the king today at Ravello, would exercise all royal prerogatives without exception.

INVASION COAST—Allied landings in France, signaling the start of the long-heralded invasion of Hitler's European Fortress, were announced this morning by General Eisenhower's headquarters German broadcasts located the center of the fighting at Caen, southeast of Le Havre where a terrific naval bombardment was reported earlier by both Allied and German sources.

Paratroops Lead Land, Sea and Air Invasion

By WES GALLAGHER

SUPREME HEADQUARTERS, Allied Expeditionary Force, June 6 (AP)—American, British and Canadian troops landed in Northern France this morning, launching the greatest overseas military operation in history with word from their supreme commander, Gen. Dwight D. Eisenhower, that "We will accept nothing except full victory" over the German masters of the Continent.

The invasion, which Eisenhower called "A Great Crusade," was announced at 7:32 a. m. Greenwich Mean Time (2:32 a. m. Central War Time) in this one-sentence communique No. 1:

"Under the command of General Eisenhower, Allied naval forces supported by strong air forces began landing Allied armies this morning on the northern coast of France."

It was announced moments later that Britain's Gen. Sir Bernard L. Montgomery, hero of the African Desert, was in charge of the assault.

The locations of the landings were not announced.

Eisenhower himself wished Godspeed to the parachutists who were the first to land on the enemy-held soil of France.

For three hours previous to the Allied announcement the German radio had been pouring forth a series of flashes reporting that the Allies were landing between Le Havre and Cherbourg along the south side of the Bay of the Seine and along the North Coast of Normandy.

This would be across the Channel and almost due south of such British ports as Hastings, Brighton, Portsmouth and Bournemouth.

The Germans also said parachutists had descended in Normandy and were being engaged by Nazi shock troops.

In a special order of the day issued to all soldiers, sailors and airmen under his command, General Eisenhower said:

"We will accept nothing except full victory."

Eisenhower told his men they were "embarking on a great crusade toward which we have striven these many months," and warned them that they facing a tough, well-prepared enemy.

Berlin said the "center of gravity" of the fierce fighting was at Caen, 30 miles southwest of Le Havre and 65 miles southeast of Cherbourg.

Caen is 10 miles inland from the sea at the base of a 75-mile-wide Normandy Peninsula.

The landings had been in progress several hours before the Allied communique was issued.

Allied soldiers leaped onto the shores which the Germans have spent nearly four years in fortifying, while Allied planes and ships hurled into those defenses barrages which the Nazis admitted were terrific.

The fleet included several battleships, which the Germans said set the whole Seine Bay area ablaze with their fire.

The Germans announced that American reinforcements began landing at dawn, aided by artificial fog, and that in some places dummy parachutists were dropped to confuse the enemy.

French patriots previously had been warned by Allied radio broadcasts to get out of areas within 35 kilometers (22 miles) of the coast to escape the shock of battle and the gigantic aerial bombardment.

The Germans said the bombers ranged as far north as Dunkirk, the unhappy port from which the beaten British army escaped almost exactly four years ago.

All England resounded with the thunder of their coming and going.

An Associated Press correspondent flying over the French coast in a B-26 Marauder reported seeing the fields inland strewn with hundreds of parachutes and dotted with gliders, while great naval forces fired into the coast fortifications.

Heavy fighting also was reported between Caen and Trouville.

One of Berlin's first claims was that the First British Parachute Division was battle-mangled.

General Montgomery, hero of the African Desert, leading the assault of the Allied Liberation Armies.

No other Allied commanders were announced, but thousands of battle-trained Allied troops, although Gen. Omar Bradley has been in command of American ground forces in England for several months.

Huge troopship armadas slipped out of English ports in the darkness and sped toward Europe where four years ago almost to the day Britain brought back the last battle-weary defenders of Dunkirk.

The Germans also declared that Calais and Dunkirk immediately across the English Channel from Britain, were under heavy air attack.

The German radio gave the first reports of the invasion while correspondents here hurriedly summoned from bed to supreme press headquarters and looked on a press conference room until the communique was released several hours after the landings were made.

It was made known at SHAEF that the supreme command felt it necessary to give the initiative in the war of words to the Germans in order to retain the initiative on land and keep the German high command in the dark as long as possible.

The great Allied armadas dwarfed anything yet seen on the sea.

Huge transport planes filled with paratroopers and pulling airborne troops in gliders roared over the German West Wall to drop their cargoes in the rear.

Berlin said that masses of Allied parachute troops had taken over Normandy, trying to seize airfields.

Just before taking off in the darkness the paratroopers were wished Godspeed by the lanky Kansas supreme commander General Eisenhower.

He was accompanied by several other of his commanders...

(Turn to Page 8, Column 4)

Caller-T...

National Archives

Soldiers, sailors and airmen of the Allied Expeditionary Force:

You are about to embark upon the great crusade toward which we have striven these
many months. The eyes of the world are upon you. The hopes and prayers of
liberty-loving people everywhere march with you.

In company with our brave Allies and brothers-in-arms on other fronts, you will bring
about the destruction of the German war machine, the elimination of Nazi tyranny over the
oppressed peoples of Europe, and security for ourselves in a free world. Your task will not be an
easy one. Your enemy is well-trained, well-equipped and battle-hardened. He will fight savagely.

But this is the year 1944! Much has happened since the Nazi triumphs of 1940-41.
The United Nations have inflicted upon the Germans great defeats, in open battle,
man-to-man. Our air offensive has seriously reduced their strength in the air
and their capacity to wage war on the ground. Our Home Fronts have given us an
overwhelming superiority in weapons and munitions of war, and placed at our
disposal great reserves of trained fighting men. The tide has turned!
The free men of the world are marching together to Victory!

I have full confidence in your courage, devotion to duty and skill in battle.
We will accept nothing less than full victory.
Good luck, and let us all beseech the blessing of Almighty God upon
this great and noble undertaking.

DWIGHT D. EISENHOWER

Supreme Allied Commander

Caller-Times file

Troops, equipment and supplies pour onto Omaha Beach days after the D-Day invasion. Operation Overlord succeeded.

Caller-Times file

Lt. Robert Edlin (left) boards a landing craft at Weymouth, England, before his troops are moved across the English Channel to participate in the D-Day invasion.

Our landings ... have failed to gain a satisfactory foothold and I have withdrawn the troops. My decision to attack at this time and place was based upon the best information available. The troops, the air and the navy did all that bravery and devotion to duty could do. If any blame or fault attaches to the attempt, it is mine alone.

— the message Gen. Eisenhower would have released if Operation Overlord had failed

Painting stripes on 'dazzle ant' ships, like this one on patrol in Kurun Harbor, Formosa, was a form of camouflage. Observers could not determine the ship's direction.

Contributed photo

Nellis Verhey (right), a paratrooper who jumped into battle on D-Day, in Frankfurt with a colleague. Verhey was a member of Gen. Dwight D. Eisenhower's personal guard.

Caller-Times file

Contributed by Lisa Baden Su

Maj. John Paul Baden, a Marine aviator, served with the 'B Sheep' Squadron in the South Pacific.

Contributed photo

Piles of ammunition and spent ammo shells testify to the heavy fire these Marines, including Loren Wesley Plummer Jr. (center) of Corpus Christi, poured into the fight for Iwo Jima in February 1945. The unprecedented brutality of the fight for the small but strategic island disturbed many who feared the Pacific war's bloodshed would intensify as the Allies neared Japan.

Contributed by James D. Robbins

Allied troops found this in Dachau, Germany.

Contributed photo

U.S. fighters soar over the Okinawa beachhead as one of the war's most savage battles rages below.

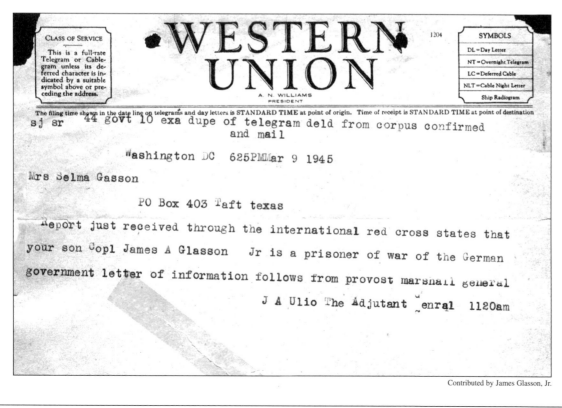

Contributed by James Glasson, Jr.

A telegram on March 9, 1945, from Washington D.C., informs Selma Glasson that her son is now a German prisoner of war.

Contributed by June Herb

Sgt. Arthur C. Berry snapped this photograph of a woman knitting amidst the ruins in Marseille, France, in March 1945.

Civic buildings in downtown Manila, Philippines, during World War II.

Contributed photo

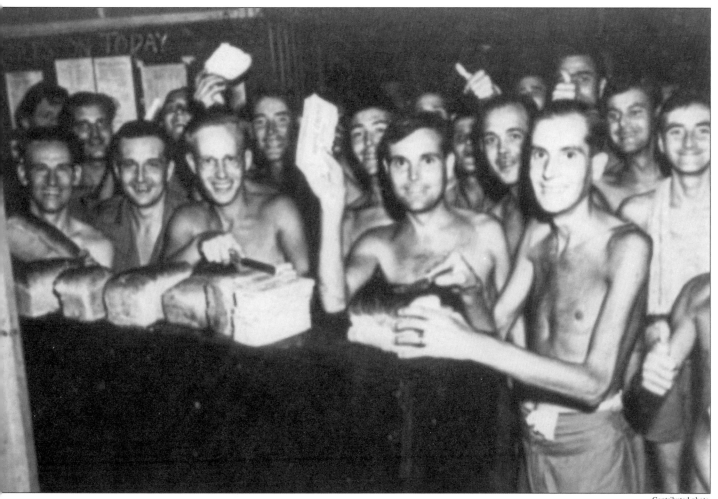

Contributed photo

…mancipated and emaciated Allied prisoners of war celebrate a decent meal in a Japanese POW camp.

Contributed photo

…risoners of war leave their prison camp. Their former Japanese guards stand in …e foreground.

Contributed photo

Prisoners of war board a ship and head home.

Contributed by Clifton Brook

When a plane crashed on the carrier, crews had to clear the flight deck of wreckage within five minutes to allow the next plane to land.

Contributed by Clifton Brooks Noel

The USS Casablanca enters Pearl Harbor and passes the USS Lexington.

Contributed by Clifton Brook

A perfect landing on an aircraft carrier as another plane comes in far behind.

Contributed by Clifton Brooks Noel

and plays for the troops aboard the USS Casablanca.

Contributed by Clifton Brooks Noel

Sailors manning their posts during general quarters take a break for lunch.

Contributed by Clifton Brooks Noel

nes are unloaded in the Philippines. Chief Clifton Brooks Noel (center) directs traffic.

Contributed by Charles Weichert

Sgt. Raymond M Weichert (left) a a friend park 'in front of the Card Red Cross Club' Reims, France, c Sept. 6, 1945.

Texas Parks & Wildlife

Army nurses, former prisoners of war, return to the United States.

Contributed photo

U.S. Marine Col. A. D. Cooley accepts the swords of surrendered Japanese officers at Taihoku, Formosa.

Raul M. Escobar in Guam in 1944. He served with the U.S. Marines from 1943 to 1948.

Contributed photo

A. Howell visits his aunts, Nellie Howell-Lege (left) and Irene Howell-Citty, in pus Christi in 1944.

Contributed by Michael A. Howell

Contributed by Doreen Harris

Air Force Lt. Thomas Allen Worsham served from 1942 to 1945.

Caller-Times

The Enola Gay, a B-29 bomber commanded by Col. Paul W. Tibbets Jr., dropped the atomic bomb on the Japanese city of Hiroshima on Aug. 6, 1945.

Contributed by James Norman Price Jr.

National Arch

Just 30 minutes before the takeoff of the Enola Gay, servicemen meet on Tinian Island. James Norman Price Jr. is sixth from the left, hands in his pockets, wearing a hat. The nose of Enola Gay is in the upper left-hand corner. A man with a movie camera films the servicemen involved in this highly secret assignment.

Col. Paul W. Tibbets Jr., pilot of the Enola Gay, waves from his cockpit prior takeoff. He is headed for Hiroshima, Japan, with an atomic bomb. Tibbets nan the plane for his mother.

U.S. leaflets dropped on Japanese cities warning civilians about the atomic bomb

TO THE JAPANESE PEOPLE:

America asks that you take immediate heed
of what we say on this leaflet.

We are in possession of the most destructive explosive
ever devised by man. A single one of our newly developed
atomic bombs is actually the equivalent in explosive
power to what 2,000 of our giant B-29s can carry on
a single mission. This awful fact is one for you to ponder
and we solemnly assure you it is grimly accurate.

We have just begun to use this weapon against your
homeland. If you still have any doubt, make inquiry
as to what happened to Hiroshima when just one
atomic bomb fell on that city.

Before using this bomb to destroy every resource of the
military by which they are prolonging this useless war, we
ask that you now petition the Emperor to end the war.
Our president has outlined for you the thirteen
consequences of an honorable surrender. We urge that
you accept these consequences and begin the work of
building a new, better and peace-loving Japan.

You should take steps now to cease military resistance.
Otherwise, we shall resolutely employ this bomb
and all our other superior weapons to promptly
and forcefully end the war.

EVACUATE YOUR CITIES.

ATTENTION JAPANESE PEOPLE:

EVACUATE YOUR CITIES.

Because your military leaders have rejected the
thirteen-part surrender declaration, two momentous
events have occurred in the last few days.

The Soviet Union, because of this rejection on the part of
the military, has notified your Ambassador Sato that it has
declared war on your nation. Thus, all powerful countries
of the world are now at war with you. Also, because of
your leaders' refusal to accept the surrender declaration
that would enable Japan to honorably end this useless
war, we have employed our atomic bomb.

A single one of our newly developed atomic bombs is actually the equivalent in explosive power to what 2,000 of our
giant B-29s could have carried on a single mission. Radio
Tokyo has told you that with the first use of this weapon of
total destruction, Hiroshima was virtually destroyed.

Before we use this bomb again and again to destroy every
resource of the military by which they are prolonging this
useless war, petition the emperor now to end the war.
Our president has outlined for you the thirteen consequences of an honorable surrender. We urge that you
accept these consequences and begin the work of building
a new, better, and peace-loving Japan.

Act at once or we shall resolutely employ this bomb
and all our other superior weapons to promptly
and forcefully end the war.

EVACUATE YOUR CITIES.

Photo and documents/The Truman Library

Contributed by Clifton Brooks N

Men in the radio room on the USS Casablanca celebrate the surrender of the Japanese.

Contributed by Clifton Brooks Noel

The Sunset of War

By Clifton Brooks Noel
Aug. 15, 1945

"At the time the war was over, we were somewhere about the middle of the vast Pacific, at a heading of due west. We were to pick up our squadron at Guam and head for the invasion of the Japanese mainland. The bridge announced that there was a terrific sunset ... and hundreds rushed to the flight deck to see this phenomenon. I had seen lots of sunsets during the war because I worked on the flight deck, but I had never seen anything like this one — happening on the very day that the war was over. It was like someone was saying, 'OK fellows, you have done a good job, but it's all over ... this is the sinking of the Rising Sun military effort of the Japanese.' "

Contributed by Clifton Brooks Noel

A plane crashed short of the USS Casablanca's flight deck and fell into the sea. The pilot freed himself from the wreckage but was pulled underwater as the plane sank. He never resurfaced. The pilot was a 24-year-old newlywed, and the war had just ended.

Contributed by Curtis M. W

This letter from Corpus Christi, postmarked Jan. 30, 1945, never reached its intended recipient, Private First Class Marvin Monroe Hall. Hall was killed in action on Feb. 3, 1945. The letter was marked 'Deceased' and returned to Mrs. Curtis Watts.

Contributed by June Herbst

The U.S. Information & Education Division distributed this book, '112 Gripes about the French,' to U.S. servicemen. This one belonged to Army Sgt. Arthur Clifton Berry.

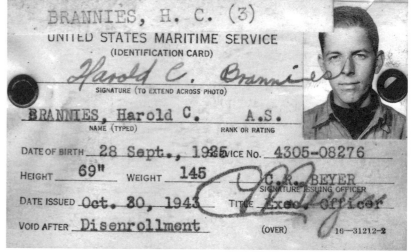

Contributed photo

An identification card for Harold C. Brannies.

Contributed by Claude D'Unger

During World War II, money in Hawaii was stamped HAWAII. If the Japanese invaded Hawaii, the money would not be legal tender anywhere else.

Contributed photo

Charles C.F. Church (left) and Lt. Sam Campbell visited the Leaning Tower of (in background) during a visit to Italy in 1945.

Caller-Times file

Edgar S. Malone (center) outside a building in Salzburg, Austria, where he helped guard political prisoners in June 1945.

Benjamin O. Davis as the first African-American general officer in the U.S. military. Brig. Gen. Davis worked for the Inspector General and for the Advisory Committee on Negro Troop Policies, uncovering many problems and weaknesses of a segregated armed forces.

National Archives

National Archives

Barbara Erickson, a member of Women Airforce Service Pilots (WASP), completed four 2,000-mile deliveries of three different types of aircraft in only about five days of flying. For her performance, she was the first WASP to be awarded the Air Medal.

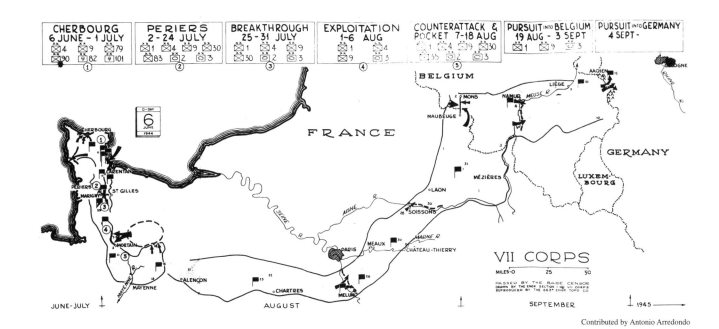

Contributed by Antonio Arredondo

Contributed by Antonio Arredondo

MERRY CHRISTMAS

Season's
Greetings
from
Germany

HAPPY NEW YEAR

Contributed by Antonio Arredondo

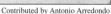

Antonio Arredondo mailed home this holiday card from Germany in 1944. It unfolded to a map
of the Allied campaigns in Europe. Arredondo served in the U.S. Army from 1943 to 1945.

Contributed by Frank 'Al' Frazier

Frank 'Al' Frazier, on the deck of the USS DeHaven, served in the Navy from 1945 to 1948 after graduating from Miller High School.

Contributed by James Norman Price, Jr.

plane carried 10,000-pound punkin bombs. Note the five hits ted on plane. This plane flew 3,000 miles from Tinian Island to bombs on Japanese targets.

Contributed by Mrs. Ben Hill

Brothers Ben T. Hill (left), of the 90th Infantry Division, 358 Service Company, and Paul R. Hill together in occupied Germany in 1945.

Caller-Times archives

Joe Dawson receives the Distinguished Service Cross from Gen. Eisenhower for his actions on D-Day.

Contributed by June Herbst

Sgt. Arthur C. Berry (standing) with friends traveling across France in 1945.

Arthur Berry (second from right) and some helpers, including a German prisoner of war (left), drag a Christmas tree to their truck at Pierra Cava, France.

Contributed photo

Contributed by Anne Armstrong

Lt. Tobin Armstrong, a fighter pilot in the U.S. Army Air Corps, was stationed outside of
Colchester, England, in the winter of 1945. One evening, as he crossed an icy bridge over a river,
a British military vehicle veered off the bridge and plunged into the water below, landing upside
down. Armstrong jumped down to the river's edge and swam to the vehicle. He freed the four
passengers and dragged them to the riverbank. Armstrong was decorated with the American
Soldier's Medal for saving the British soldiers. His wife was appointed U.S. ambassador to
England from 1976 to 1977, and she remembers that his reputation made her job much easier.

Contributed by Joe L. Quintanilla

In Dec. 1947, the Quintanilla brothers lined up for a portrait. From left, Sgt. Navidad Quintanilla (who participated in the Normandy invasion), Cpl. Frank Quintanilla (who served in 1944 and 1945), Pfc. Gilbert Quintanilla (in the framed photograph, who was killed in France in 1944), Pfc. Jesus Quintanilla (who served in the Army in 1946 and 1947), Sgt Jose Quintanilla (who served in the Air Force from 1947 to 1950) and Sgt. Manuel Quintanilla (in oval photo, who served in the Marine Corps from 1954 to 1958).

Frederick George (Jack) Culbertson Jr. was overseas for three years and did not see his daughter until she was 2½ years old. He served in North Africa, France and Germany. In this portrait are Martha Brown Culbertson (from left), Cathryn Lynn Culbertson and Frederick George Culbertson, Jr.

Contributed by Martha Culbertson

Lt. Robert Vernon Poe Sr. (right), a naval aviator, served on the aircraft carrier USS Midway. He was killed in a crash in June 1949.

Contributed by Robert Poe Jr.

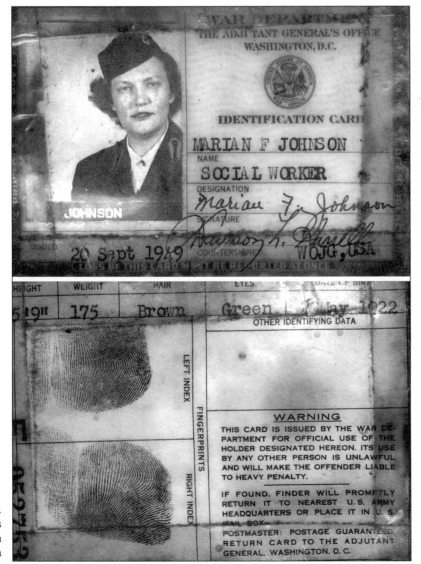

Marian F. Johnson's identification card. She was a social worker.

Contributed photo

Contributed by Carol Ann Zeitler

Home on leave

T.M. Jarvis Jr. served in World War II. He was injured in the Hurtgen Forest. Because he was the first double amputee war veteran to return to Corpus Christi, the people of the city built a home for the Jarvis family. It was built in one day, on March 9, 1946. 'In spite of my father's handicap, he led a full and happy life. He wore artificial legs for 51 years and was a joy and an inspiration to many of us. He certainly was a hero to our family and I appreciate the opportunity to have him included in your book.'

Contributed by Shawn Bodine

Veterans of the February 1945 Battle of Iwo Jima at a ceremony in Sherrill Park in 2003.

Contributed by Mrs. Ben Hill

A Belgian memorial plaque honors the soldiers
of the U.S. 90th Infantry Division.

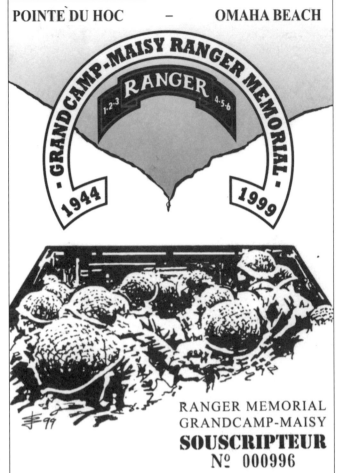

POINTE DU HOC — OMAHA BEACH

RANGER MEMORIAL
GRANDCAMP-MAISY
SOUSCRIPTEUR
№ 000996

Contributed by Robert Edlin

A card like this one permitted veterans and visitors to participate in the inauguration of the Grandcamp-Maisy Ranger Memorial on June 6, 1999. The Normandy Allies Association sponsored the event, which was held on the 55th annivesary of Operation Overlord, to commemorate the heroism of U.S. soldiers.

George Gongora/Caller-Times file

Robert Edlin, a decorated Army Ranger, with a piece of furniture from the area of France where he served on D-Day.

George Storms (left) and Edgar S. Malone display their war souvenirs from France and Germany, including a red Nazi armband, a map illustrating the fighting their artillery unit participated in, and various weapons and ribbons.

George Tuley/Caller-Times file

Caller-Times file

Nellis Verhey in 1994.

EXECUTIVE ORDER 9981

Establishing the President's Committee on Equality of Treatment and Opportunity in the Armed Forces

WHEREAS it is essential that there be maintained in the armed services of the United States the highest standards of democracy, with equality of treatment and opportunity for all those who serve in our country's defense:

NOW THEREFORE, by virtue of the authority vested in me as President of the United States, by the Constitution and the statutes of the United States, and as Commander in Chief of the armed services, it is hereby ordered as follows:

1. It is hereby declared to be the policy of the President that there shall be equality of treatment and opportunity for all persons in the armed services without regard to race, color, religion or national origin. This policy shall be put into effect as rapidly as possible, having due regard to the time required to effectuate any necessary changes without impairing efficiency or morale.

2. There shall be created in the National Military Establishment an advisory committee to be known as the President's Committee on Equality of Treatment and Opportunity in the Armed Services, which shall be composed of seven members to be designated by the President.

3. The Committee is authorized on behalf of the President to examine into the rules, procedures and practices of the Armed Services in order to determine in what respect such rules, procedures and practices may be altered or improved with a view to carrying out the policy of this order. The Committee shall confer and advise the Secretary of Defense, the Secretary of the Army, the Secretary of the Navy, and the Secretary of the Air Force, and shall make such recommendations to the President and to said Secretaries as in the judgment of the Committee will effectuate the policy hereof.

4. All executive departments and agencies of the Federal Government are authorized and directed to cooperate with the Committee in its work, and to furnish the Committee such information or the services of such persons as the Committee may require in the performance of its duties.

5. When requested by the Committee to do so, persons in the armed services or in any of the executive departments and agencies of the Federal Government shall testify before the Committee and shall make available for use of the Committee such documents and other information as the Committee may require.

6. The Committee shall continue to exist until such time as the President shall terminate its existence by Executive order.

HARRY S. TRUMAN

The White House
July 26, 1948

Korea

Korean War Timeline

Truman

MacArthur

Walker

MacArthur at Inchon

Truman and MacArthur

1950

More than 90,000 North Korean troops cross the 38th Parallel, the border between North and South Korea. The Korean War begins.

U.S. President HARRY S. TRUMAN moves U.S. warships to the Far East region to bolster security.

The United Nations condemns North Korea's actions.

Truman directs **General of the Army DOUGLAS MacARTHUR,** the commander of the Japanese occupation, to assist the South Koreans with all forces available to him. MacArthur turns to the 8th U.S. Army in Japan and additional forces in Hawaii and Okinawa.

The U.N. asks member nations to provide military aid to turn the tide in South Korea. The United Nations Command is created and MacArthur is named its commander.

MacArthur gives command of the 8th U.S. Army to **Lt. Gen. WALTON H. WALKER,** who also takes command of the South Korean armies.

Task Force Smith, made up of elements of infantry and artillery, arrives in Korea with more than 500 soldiers to help the Republic of Korea troops.

First land battle, the Battle of Osan, begins. Task Force Smith stalls North Korean attackers, but the Allies are soon pushed south to the port city of Pusan.

From early August to mid-September, more than 84,000 U.S. troops under Walker's command successfully defend the 140 miles of the Pusan perimeter.

MacArthur successfully executes **OPERATION CHROMITE,** the Allied landing at Inchon.

The 8th U.S. Army breaks out of the Pusan perimeter and heads north.

Truman authorizes MacArthur to move his forces north of the 38th Parallel into North Korea, as long as there are no Chinese or Soviet countermoves.

Truman and MacArthur meet in person at Wake Island. Truman asks MacArthur if the Chinese will enter the war. MacArthur assures him they will not, and if they do, he says, "I will make of them the greatest slaughter in the history of warfare."

Chinese troops enter the war. As Allied troops prepare to celebrate victory in Korea, Chinese troops launch a surprise counteroffensive in North Korea on Dec. 15. MacArthur blames the surprise on the failure of U.S. intelligence agencies.

MacArthur bristles over the restrictions

Ridgway

Van Fleet

Clark

Taylor

Washington places on his operations ou of fear of the Korean War expanding into China and the Soviet Union.

The Battle of Changjin (Chosin) Reservoir begins, where U.S. Marines are surrounded and fight their way to the Korea an coast.

Lt. Gen. Walker is killed in an automobile accident. Command of the 8th Army passes to **Lt. Gen. MATTHEW B. RIDGWAY.**

The U.S. Navy evacuates 100,000 U.S. an South Korean troops the day before Christmas.

1951

Seoul falls to communist troops.

The Chinese attack again with 500,000 sol diers, pounding Allied troops south for 50 miles. In three months, Allied and U.S. troops have fallen back 300 miles, the longest retreat in U.S. history.

The U.S. Navy begins Wonsan siege. The city will not fall for 860 days, the longest successful siege of a port in U.S. history.

Ridgway counterattacks the communist offensive with Operation Ripper, driving the Chinese and the North Koreans back to the 38th parallel and recovering Seoul

In April, the Chinese hurl 250,000 men at the U.N. allies, leading to the war's biggest battle.

Truman relieves MacArthur for the general's continued criticism of national policy. Ridgway replaces him a U.N. commander. **Lt. Gen. JAMES VAN FLEET** assumes command of the 8th Army.

Allied troops fight the battles of Bloody Ridge for Hill 983 and Heartbreak Ridg for Hill 931.

Korean War truce talks begin on July 10.

1952

Gen. MARK CLARK assumes command of U.N. forces in Korea. Fighting dies down into a violent stalemate.

1953

Lt. Gen. MAXWELL D. TAYLOR replaces Gen. Van Fleet.

Armistice is signed on July 27. All fighting stops. Total Allied casualties exceed 500,000, with 95,000 dead, including 34,000 U.S. deaths. Communist casualties, including POWs, are more than 1,500,000. The stalemate remains today.

Sources: PBS.org, Naval Historical Center, and the U.S. Arm

President Harry S. Truman outlines a new world in the shadow of the Cold War.

March 12, 1947

The gravity of the situation which confronts the world today necessitates my appearance before a joint session of the Congress. The foreign policy and the national security of this country are involved. ...

e aspect of the present situation, which I wish to present to you at this time for your sideration and decision, concerns Greece and Turkey. ...

e of the primary objectives of the foreign policy of the United States is the creation conditions in which we and other nations will be able to work out a way of life free m coercion. This was a fundamental issue in the war with Germany and Japan. Our tory was won over countries which sought to impose their will, and their way of life, on other nations. ...

the present moment in world history nearly every nation must choose between alter-ive ways of life. The choice is too often not a free one. One way of life is based upon will of the majority, and is distinguished by free institutions, representative govern-nt, free elections, guarantees of individual liberty, freedom of speech and religion, I freedom from political oppression. The second way of life is based upon the will of inority forcibly imposed upon the majority. It relies upon terror and oppression, a trolled press and radio; fixed elections, and the suppression of personal freedoms.

elieve that it must be the policy of the United States to support free peoples who are isting attempted subjugation by armed minorities or by outside pressures. I believe t we must assist free peoples to work out their own destinies in their own way. I ieve that our help should be primarily through economic and financial aid which is ential to economic stability and orderly political processes.

s necessary only to glance at a map to realize that the survival and integrity of the ek nation are of grave importance in a much wider situation. If Greece should fall ler the control of an armed minority, the effect upon its neighbor, Turkey, would be nediate and serious. Confusion and disorder might well spread throughout the entire ddle East.

must take immediate and resolute action. I therefore ask the Congress to provide hority for assistance to Greece and Turkey in the amount of $400,000,000 for the iod ending June 30, 1948. ... In addition to funds, I ask the Congress to authorize the ail of American civilian and military personnel to Greece and Turkey, at the request those countries, to assist in the tasks of reconstruction, and for the purpose of super-ing the use of such financial and material assistance as may be furnished. ...

e seeds of totalitarian regimes are nurtured by misery and want. They spread and w in the evil soil of poverty and strife. They reach their full growth when the hope a people for a better life has died. We must keep that hope alive.

e free peoples of the world look to us for support in maintaining their freedoms. If falter in our leadership, we may endanger the peace of the world — and we shall ely endanger the welfare of our own nation. Great responsibilities have been placed on us by the swift movement of events.

m confident that the Congress will face these responsibilities squarely.

ce: Truman Presidential Library and Museum

Caller-Times file

Truman's new doctrine divided the world between the free and the oppressed, between allies of the U.S. and allies of the Soviet Union.

The Corpus Christi Times

WARM

FINAL EDITION

VOLUME 40—NO. 306 — Entered as second class matter at the post office at Corpus Christi, Texas, under the Act of March 3, 1879 — CORPUS CHRISTI, TEXAS, TUESDAY, JUNE 27, 1950 — Published every week day afternoon by The Caller-Times Publishing Co — Twenty-Four Pages Today—PRICE FIVE CENTS

U. S. AIRFORCE, FLEET ORDERED INTO FIGHT

NAM OFFICIAL HERE—W. R. Archer of Houston, (second from left) will give the principle address at the National Association of Manufacturers banquet tonight on the White Plaza Hotel Deck. Pictured with him are T. Frank Smith, a local radio station official and head of the current Chamber of Commerce drive, and J. F. Morton, manager of the Corn Products Refining Co. plant here; and C. E. Russell, operator of the Automotive Supply and Machine Shop here. Russell also will speak at tonight's meeting.

'BRIGHTEST SPOT ON EARTH'

NAM Vice President Lauds Gulf Coast Area

By MARY MAHONEY

The critical situation in Korea today was termed "a terrible indictment on the part of America" by W. R. Archer, Houston grain man and vice president of the National Association of Manufacturers.

"We have permitted communism to spread in Korea while concentrating on ways to stamp out its program in Europe," Archer declared here today. "Thousands of dollars have been spent in an attempt to check communism at home and in Europe, but we have been woefully lax in other areas where our help has been sorely needed."

Gulf Coast 'Brightest Spot'

Archer is in Corpus Christi to speak at a meeting of the National Association of Manufacturers at 8:30 o'clock tonight at the White Plaza Hotel Deck. His talk tonight will concern the effects of recent legislative, political and economic events.

The Houston grain man, who served on the agricultural committee of the Chamber of Commerce at Houston for seven years, said this morning that "Texas, and especially the Gulf Coast area of the state, is the brightest spot on earth today."

"This is a tremendous state, and it has all sorts of possibilities for future industrial and agricultural expansion," Archer stated.

"It has a diversified agriculture economy, which lends itself to future growth, its port cities have a wonderful future in world commerce, and the state has enough raw materials to produce products for world trade."

Commenting on Corpus Christi's growth during the next few years, Archer said, "There is no reason why the city should not grow to eight or 10 times its present size. Like the Houston area, this city has just about everything it needs in its own immediate area."

Business in Houston

Archer went to Houston just after World War I. He opened an office

(See ARCHER, Page 12.)

USED CAR DEALERS SUPPORTING AMEY

Wire to Governor Praises Motor Vehicle Registration Chief; Shivers Checking

Corpus Christi Used Car Dealers Association this morning wired Gov. Allen Shivers of their willingness to "fight by the side of E. J. Amey," director of the State Highway Department, motor vehicle registration, and told the governor that his official investigation has begun on the dealers' request for Amey's removal.

Used Car Dealers Satisfied

The used car dealers wire was sent by J. S. Keetch, president of the used car dealers group here, and B. J. Hammock, vice president, after they learned that Jones' group had requested Amey's removal.

Hammock said this morning that the used car dealers association did not want the public, or the governor to think that the request for Amey's removal came from all the car dealers of Texas. "It was only from the new car dealers," Hammock said, "and the used car dealers of Corpus Christi and of Texas do not feel that way."

"We have been informed of a telegram to the governor of the State of Texas asking for the immediate dismissal of E. J. Amey, director of the Motor Vehicle Division. This dismissal, according to the morning edition of The Corpus Christi Caller, was asked, and we quote from the above mentioned paper by the Texas Automobile Dealers Association.

Clarification Sought

"This matter should be clarified. The dismissal of E. J. Amey is asked by the New Car Dealers Association of Texas and of Corpus Christi of which there are approximately 17 members in the Corpus Christi association, and does not constitute the opinion of the Texas Used Car Dealers Association and the Corpus Christi Used Car Dealers Association, of which there are in the excess of 390 members.

"In the opinion of the Texas Used Car Dealers Association and the Corpus Christi Used Car Dealers Association, Mr. E. J. Amey has done a wonderful job in performing his duties as a public servant to the citizens and automobile buyers of the State of Texas, and in the residence of other states that have moved to Texas, and have been required by law to register.

(See DEALERS, Page 12.)

Campbell First Witness in Trial Of Pappageorge

H. D. Campbell, former game warden now employed as a peace officer on the Padre Island causeway, was the first witness this morning in the trial of George Pappageorge, charged with illegal possession of a seine enclosed waters of Laguna Madre.

County Atty. James C. Martin, prosecutor, called Campbell to testify before Judge Green Moffet in county court at law as the arresting officer when Pappageorge was taken into custody on Dec. 1, 1949 at Boat Hole in the laguna. Campbell said that he observed Pappageorge's boat as it approached the Boat Hole from a point near Pita Island, and that when Pappageorge tied up at the pier, Campbell boarded the boat. Wet Seine on Boat

He said he found on the boat a wet drag seine, and a box which he estimated would hold between 1,200 and 1,600 pounds of fish. Campbell said he arrested Pappageorge and charged him on Dec. 5 before Justice of the Peace W. A. Gilleland with illegal possession of the seine.

Under cross-examination by Fairee P. Wade, defense attorney,

(See TRIAL, Page 12.)

INVESTIGATES COMPLAINTS

Judge Allred Unexpected Luncheon Guest at Jail

Federal prisoners in county jail today had an unexpected guest at lunch — Judge James V. Allred, who, less than an hour before in federal district court had sentenced 13 of them for unlawful entry into the United States.

Judge Allred decided to make the informal call after an alien, sentenced to a short term in the jail, had requested the court to give him a penitentiary sentence instead because, he said: "They do not give much to eat in the jail."

It was the second time this month the same request had been made by a prisoner.

Judge Allred arrived just a minute late to eat with the prisoners, but he was served a bowl of beans from the prisoners themselves that they had cornbread and spaghetti.

"The beans were all right," Judge Allred said. "I happen to like them."

Prisoners had complained, mostly about quantity rather than quality. The judge said he could not say after the one visit whether the diet was insufficient.

"You can't afford to go alone by what the prisoners say," he explained. "But after two complaints, it seemed worth an investigation."

U.S. Bombing Of Korea May Begin Tonight

American-Trained Troops Push Reds Back North of Seoul

TOKYO, Wednesday, June 28.—(AP)— Decision to send American-manned bombers to drive the invading Communists out of South Korea and appointment of an American general to command a joint defense operation" were reported early today.

An apparently well-founded report from a source which cannot be identified said American planes "tonight" would begin bombing all towns captured by the North Koreans who invaded South Korea Sunday.

(Part of this dispatch was timed just before midnight, and part after midnight. "Tonight" could mean in darkness Wednesday morning or Wednesday night.)

General Reported Named

Early today a Seoul broadcast quoted President Syngman Rhee as announcing that "Gen. Church" has been named to command a "joint defense operation" and that Gen. MacArthur has promised the South Koreans bombers and anti-tank guns.

The Gen. Church referred to was apparently Brig. Gen. John H. Church, listed as occupation headquarters as commander of the Tsukyus (Okinawa) military government.

There was no immediate confirmation at headquarters of such an appointment. The Seoul broadcast was heard by two different agencies in Tokyo and was in line with the trend of the Korean crisis.

(See WARFRONT, Page 12.)

ONE-YEAR DRAFT EXTENSION VOTED

WASHINGTON, June 27.—(AP)— Senate-House conference today voted a one-year extension of the President's expiring power to draft young men.

The agreement, which must be ratified by both chambers, also would empower the President to order the National Guard and reserves to immediate active duty.

The Senate-House conference obviously acted because of the tense Korean situation.

They junked previous restrictions voted by the Senate and House upon presidential authority to induct manpower and voted out a one year extension of existing draft powers.

Sen. Byrd (D-Va), one of the conferees, told a reporter that the previously deadlocked lawmakers had quickly agreed today that this was no time to have the world think there was a dispute here over such a matter.

Yesterday's high for Texas was 107 degrees at Presidio. Other high temperatures were Rio Grande City 108, Wink and El Paso 102, Laredo and Childress 101 and Lubbock 100. Galveston reported the lowest reading — 52.

Only rainfall was .10 inch in Dalhart.

(See DRAFT, Page 12.)

U.S. Has 500 AF Planes, 18 Warships in Pacific

WASHINGTON, June 27. (AP)—The United States has 500 plus Air Force planes and 18 warships in the Far Pacific, U. S. military manpower there totals 125,500.

Defense Department officials supplied the figures today.

The Air Force says it has six fighter groups, one medium bomber group and two light bomber squadrons ready for action.

The fleet units are: The heavy cruiser Rochester, six destroyers, two escort destroyers, three submarines, a high speed transport, a minelayer and a seaplane tender.

Other U. S. naval forces in the Western Pacific include five war ships based on Japan under Vice Adm. Calvin T. Joy. These are the light anti-aircraft cruiser Juneau and four destroyers.

There are four divisions of Army ground troops in the area.

MacArthur Got Order Last Night

WASHINGTON, June 27. (AP)— The Army said today that President Truman's order for air and sea support of South Korean troops was passed last night to Gen. Douglas MacArthur, who has supreme command of all the U. S. forces in the Far Pacific.

A spokesman said the order became effective during a long telephone conference which began at 4:12 p.m. last night between Pentagon officials and MacArthur.

Air National Guard Units Under Alerts

WASHINGTON, June 27. (AP)— The Air Force said today commanders of a number of Air National Guard units alerted their men at news of the outbreak of fighting in Korea.

An Air Force spokesman said the weekend alerts were precautionary measures taken on the initiative of the unit commanders to assure that the units were in touch with all of their personnel.

France Still Minus Cabinet

PARIS, June 27. (AP)— Former Premier Henri Queuille abandoned his hope today of forming a new French government.

With the French president vested in his third day, Queuille was unable to persuade the Socialist Party to rejoin a coalition cabinet dedicated against the Communists.

Some political observers expressed belief that Queuille, because of his refusal of a firm assurance from the Radical Socialist Chiefs party would try again to form a cabinet.

Truman Sending Strong Aid to South Korea

WASHINGTON, June 27. (AP)— President Truman today ordered United States planes and warships to the aid of South Korean forces. He laid down a policy of standing firm against Communist aggression in the far Pacific.

As a part of the broader policy, Mr. Truman directed that the U. S. Seventh Fleet be prepared to intervene to prevent any Communist attack on Formosa, the island refuge of the Chinese Nationalist government.

SITUATION IN BRIEF

WASHINGTON — President Truman orders United States planes and warships to aid South Korean forces, in broad policy of firmness in far Pacific. President directs fleet to intervene against any Communist invasion of Formosa orders increased aid to Philippines, Indochina, but asks Chiang Kai-shek to cease attacks on Chinese mainland.

TOKYO — American fighters shoot down four Communist planes interfering with refugee airlift. Communists reported pushed back 20 miles from Seoul by resurgent republican forces.

TAKE SUCCESS — U. S. prepares important Korean resolution for UN Security Council meeting on Korean conflict. Soviet and U. S. delegates meet at secret luncheon before afternoon Security session.

ITAZUKI AIRBASE — Kyushu, Japan — American military transports, shielded by fighters, flying out more than 564 U. S. personnel from American Seoul. About 250 U. S. military advisers remain, driving south in motorized equipment to keep contact with southern army, U. S. Ambassador John J. Muccio reported them out.

MOSCOW — Soviet press withholds publishes Tass reports saying de Gaulle (Soviet) meeting at which resolution ordered and legal because Soviet Union not present.

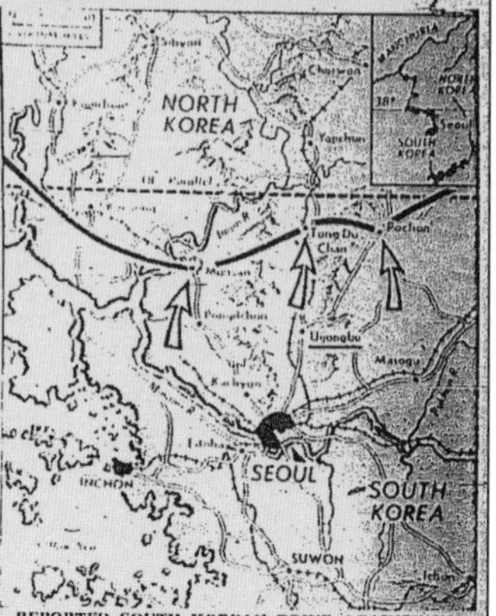

Americans Down 4 Korean Planes

TOKYO, June 27. (P) — U. S. manned fighters today shot down four North Korean planes attempting to disrupt the evacuation of Americans from South Korea, it was learned tonight.

There was no official announcement of the action from Gen. MacArthur's headquarters. But reports gathered by correspondents at Itazuki airbase in southern Japan, terminus of the airlift, bore out the figures.

MacArthur's headquarters officially announced earlier in the day that one American fighter had shot

(See TRUMAN, Page 12.)

MANY RUMORS CIRCULATE

No Local Enlistment Rush As Result of Korea Crisis

The tense situation in Korea which circulated every type of rumor conceivable in Corpus Christi did not stir up an immediate reaction among potential enlistees in the armed forces, local recruiting officers reported this morning.

NAS Not Alerted

Enlistments were following the same ratio of one or two a day at the Navy, Marine, Army and Air Force recruiting centers these mornings. The Army and Air

7th Fleet Units Move

HONG KONG, June 27. (UP)— Three units of the U. S. Seventh Fleet left Hong Kong for an undisclosed destination today, cutting short a three-day recreational visit.

They were the destroyer Maddox, the destroyer escort S. N. Moore, and the submarine Cabezon.

Force station said that they had received a few inquiries from former officers about now, they might regain their old status, but that was the only information they had that the international situation had changed.

Officials at the Public Information Offices at the Naval Air Station said they had received a few inquiries from civilians asking if the station had been alerted in any way, but could only reply that they only knew when they read in the paper or heard on the radio.

Many Calls to Caller-Times

Meanwhile the The Caller-Times editorial room continued requests for briefing on the current situation kept telephones busy, particularly in the late morning. Many of the requests sought confirmation of rumors they had heard.

The switchboard said that the calls for information reached a 12 or 20 an hour peak between 11 a.m. and noon.

TEXT OF TRUMAN STATEMENT

WASHINGTON, June 27. (AP)— The text of President Truman's statement today on Korea:

In Korea the government forces, which were armed to prevent border raids and to preserve internal security, were attacked by invading forces from North Korea. The Security Council of the United Nations called upon the invading troops to cease hostilities and to withdraw to the 38th parallel. This they have not done, but on the contrary have pressed the attack. The Security Council called upon all members of the United Nations to render every assistance to the United Nations in the execution of this resolution.

In these circumstances I have ordered United States air and sea forces to give the Korean government troops cover and support.

The attack upon Korea makes it plain beyond all doubt that communism has passed beyond the use of subversion to conquer independent nations and will now use armed invasion and war.

It has defied the orders of the Security Council of the United Nations issued to preserve international peace and security. In these circumstances the occupation of Formosa by Communist forces would be a direct threat to the security of the Pacific area and to United States forces performing their lawful and necessary functions in that area.

Accordingly I have ordered the Seventh Fleet to prevent any attack on Formosa. As a corollary of this action I am calling upon the Chinese government on Formosa to cease all air and sea operations against the mainland. The 7th Fleet will see that this is done. The determination of the future status of Formosa must await the restoration of security in the Pacific, a peace settlement with Japan, or consideration by the United Nations.

I have also directed that United States forces in the Philippines be strengthened and that military assistance to the Philippines government be accelerated.

I know that all members of the United Nations will consider carefully the consequences of this latest aggression in Korea in defiance of the charter of the United Nations. A return to the rule of force in international affairs would have far reaching effects. The United States will continue to uphold the rule of law.

I have instructed Ambassador Austin, as the representative of the United States to the Security Council, to report these steps to the Council.

Stock Market Losses Halted

NEW YORK, June 27. (P)— Selling forces battered the stock market for the second day in a row today after yesterday's disclosed a new hard-hitting policy in the Far East.

Final prices were down $1 to $2 a share but well above the lows for the session. Some stocks closed higher. Losses at one time amounted to a peak of more than $7 each.

Continued Warm Weather Forecast Through Tomorrow

Continued warm weather for Corpus Christi and vicinity through tomorrow was forecast today by the U. S. Weather Bureau.

Prospects of scattered showers previously forecast for tomorrow morning appears to have dissipated, the bureau said.

Sailing will be favorable before light southeasterly winds tonight and tomorrow morning. Winds will rise to 12 to 14 miles an hour tomorrow afternoon.

High temperature expected tomorrow is 91 to 96 degrees, the low tonight will be 75.

Temperatures were expected to be around the low-degree mark in most of the state today.

WEATHER

Forecast for Corpus Christi and vicinity: Continued warm through Wednesday.

Low temperature tonight 75; high tomorrow 91 to 96.

Sailing weather. Favorable before light southeasterly winds tonight, becoming 12 to 14 miles per hour tomorrow afternoon.

High temperature yesterday 94; low this morning 72.

Sunrise 5:36 a. m. Wednesday; sunset 7:20 p.m. Tuesday; moonrise 6:50 p.m. Wednesday; moonset 3:37 a.m. Wednesday.

(Additional weather data on Page 12.)

Negro Quintuplets Only Live 4 Hours

NEW ORLEANS, June 27.—(P)— Quintuplets, four boys and a girl, were born to a 24-year-old Negro girl here today, but all died within four hours of births.

Caller-Times archives

REPORTED SOUTH KOREAN DRIVE AGAINST INVADERS—South Korean forces (arrows), mounting a counter-offensive against the Communist invaders from the north, today were reported to have pushed back the North Koreans to a line running approximately below Kaesong and Munsan on the west to Tong Du Chan and Pochon on the east. Reports indicate that the important town of Uijongbu, 12 miles north of Seoul, the capital, has been recaptured. (AP Wirephoto)

National Archives

U.S. infantrymen comfort each other when a friend is killed in the Haktong-ni region on Aug. 28, 1950. Behind them, a medical corpsman prepares casualty tags.

National Archives

Troops of the 1st Marine Division guard captured Chinese soldiers during fighting at Hoengsong, Korea, on March 2, 1951.

Contributed by Mihoko Pittd

Army Cpl. Alton J. 'Charlie' Pittdman and Miho 'Mike' Tai were married in Tokyo, Japan, on Aug. 1951, during the Korean War. Pittdman served in Army from 1947 to 1953. Pittdman died on May 2003. The couple was married for 52 years.

Contributed p

Leroy Blount Blanton served in the U.S. Army. He enl ed in 1940 and was discharged in 1964. His tour took h to Korea.

Contributed by Janice C. Phillips

Pvt. Brian E. O'Brien walks along the Korean demilitarized zone in 1953.

Contributed by Diana M. Gonzales

he Lemos brothers in Corpus Christi in 1951. From left, Robert G. Lemos, Mel G. Lemos, James G. Lemos and Frank G. Lemos.

Contributed photo

Friends from Corpus Christi in Seoul, South Korea, on Nov. 1, 1957. Top (from left): Joe Rivas and Juan Jose Silva, Jr. Bottom (from left): Robert Puente, Roland Leal and Ray Gonzalez.

Contributed by Edwin Lawrence Harvin Jr.

Lt. Cmdr. Edwin Lawrence Harvin Jr. on board the USS Wallace L. Lind, DD-703, off the Korean coast in 1951. Harvin served in the naval reserve from 1942 to 1946, and he was recalled to service from 1951 to 1990.

Contributed photo

Paul Eubanks in flight school in 1953. He served in the U.S. Navy from 1953 to 1975 and retired as a lieutenant commander.

Privates first class and friends Harry Swift and Robert Placid, both in the 24th Infantry (Victory) Division, enjoy the luxury of a shave before going on patrol in Korea in 1952. 'How wonderful it is to shave once again with facilities such as these,' one of them writes.

Contributed by Sylvia Swift

Contributed by Juan Reyes

ny MPs display their weapons. Corpus Christi native Private First Class Juan Reyes (center) and fellow MPs in Yong Chon, Korea.

Contributed photo

ter Cameron Jones served in the U.S. Navy. He enlisted in 1952 and was
harged in 1956. His tour took him to Korea. His highest rank was AD3,
his decorations include the National Defense Medal, Korean War Medal
the Korean Service Medal.

Contributed by Sandra Duron Rosas

Master Sgt. Jose I. Duron dressed warmly to endure the Korean winter.

Contributed by Bob Mill

Marine Private First Class Bob Miller (right) and a friend chat with a runner-up to 1962's Miss America (left) and 1962's Miss America Mary Beale Fletcher in Coronado, Calif.

Army Spc. 4 Nicholas R. Ramirez was stationed in Germany in 1960. He's smiling because he's just been handed his discharge orders, and in 15 days he will no longer be in the Army.

Contributed by Nicholas Ramirez

Contributed by John and Dovie Mc

Air Force Maj. Gen. W.P. McBride was sketched in Thailand in 1968. He rece the Distinguished Flying Cross from the British Government for his actions in Korean War. He also received the French Croix de Guerre. He served from to 1973.

Vietnam

Vietnam War Timeline

Ho Chi Minh

Eisenhower

Diem

Kennedy

Johnson

Johnson takes the oath.

1945 — 1957

Japanese in Vietnam surrender to Allies. Communist activist **HO CHI MINH** creates a provisional government and declares the independence of Vietnam.

British forces take Saigon and hand power in Vietnam to the French.

Ho's Vietminh troops kill the first American victim of the war — an intelligence agent driving to the airport — possibly by accident.

The Indochina War begins when the Democratic Republic of Vietnam attacks French forces.

Soviet Union and China offer assistance to Ho Chi Minh. The U.S. provides $15 million, including military advisers, to the French for their war in Vietnam.

40,000 Vietminh troops surround French forces at Dienbienphu and defeat them.

U.S. President DWIGHT D. EISENHOWER presents the Domino Theory, explaining how communism can topple one government after another.

Geneva Convention begins. The French and the Vietminh agree to end hostilities, and Vietnam is divided. Ho will control the north and **NGO DINH DIEM** will control the south.

Diem is elected president of the Republic of Vietnam, and the U.S. sends more military advisers.

1960 — 1963

JOHN F. KENNEDY defeats Vice President Richard Nixon for the presidency.

National Liberation Front for South Vietnam organized. Diem calls them the Vietcong.

Vice President LYNDON B. JOHNSON assures Diem of U.S. support and calls him 'the Churchill of Asia.'

Defoliant Agent Orange used for the first time in Vietnam.

Kennedy approves a military overthrow of Diem's government. Diem is shot to death. Just weeks later, Kennedy is assassinated in Dallas. **Lyndon B. Johnson becomes president.**

1964 — 1967

USS Maddox reports North Vietnamese gunboats have fired on the destroyer in the Gulf of Tonkin.

President Johnson asks Congress to authorize the Gulf of Tonkin resolution, which allows him to wage war on North Vietnam without a declaration of war.

Johnson is re-elected by one of the greatest landslides in American history.

Operation Rolling Thunder — the sustained

McNamara

Westmoreland

Nixon

Kissinger

Ford

bombing of North Vietnam — begins.

Defense Secretary ROBERT McNAMARA testifies to Congress that U.S. efforts against the North Vietnamese have been ineffective.

1968

North Vietnam launches the Tet Offensive and is thrown back. Although it was a major military victory for the U.S., man question the overall gains of the war.

U.S. commander in Vietnam **Gen. WILLIAM WESTMORELAN** asks for 200,000 more troops.

U.S. troops slaughter villagers in My Lai.

Johnson announces he won't run for re-election.

Paris Peace Talks between the U.S. and North Vietnam begin.

RICHARD NIXON defeats Vice Preside Hubert Humphrey for the presidency.

1969 — 1973

Nixon begins Operation Breakfast — the secret bombing of Cambodia to destroy Communist base camps.

Ho Chi Minh dies.

Anti-war demonstrations in Washington, D.C., are bigger than ever before.

National Guardsmen open fire on student anti-war protestors at Kent State University in Ohio, killing four.

The Pentagon Papers, an analysis of U.S. involvement in Vietnam, are smuggled and published in *The New York Times*.

Nixon reduces troops strength in Vietnam by 70,000. B-52s bomb Hanoi.

National Security Advisor HENRY KISSINGER declares that Paris Peace Talks are successful. He'll win the Nobel Peace Prize for his effort to effect a cease-fire.

Nixon is re-elected, and the last U.S. troo leave Vietnam.

1974

Civil war in Vietnam re-ignites.

Nixon impeachment hearings begin. Amor the charges: the bombing of Cambodia. Nixon resigns. **Vice President GERAI R. FORD** becomes president.

1975

Communist offensive begins, slowly pushing back South Vietnamese forces

Saigon falls to the North Vietnamese.

Sources: PBS, the John F. Kennedy Library and Museum, Lyndon Baines Johnson Presidential Library and Museum, Nixon Presidential Materials Staff, the Gerald R. Ford Pres tial Library and Museum

Lyndon Baines Johnson Presidential Library and Museum

President Lyndon B. Johnson's Message to Congress
Aug. 5, 1964

Last night I announced to the American people the North Vietnamese regime had conducted further deliberate attacks against U.S. naval vessels operating in international waters, and that I had therefore directed air action against gunboats and supporting facilities used in theses hostile operations. This air action has now been carried out with substantial damage to the boats and facilities. Two U.S. aircraft were lost in the action. ...

These latest actions of the North Vietnamese regime have given a new and grave turn to the already serious situation in southeast Asia. ...

Our policy in southeast Asia has been consistent and unchanged since 1954. I summarized it on June 2, in four simple propositions:

1. America keeps her word. Here as elsewhere, we must and shall honor our commitments.
2. The issue is the future of southeast Asia as a whole. A threat to any nation in that region is a threat to all, and a threat to us.
3. Our purpose is peace. We have no military, political, or territorial ambitions in the area.
4. This is not a jungle war, but a struggle for freedom on every front of human activity. Our military and economic assistance to South Vietnam and Laos in particular has the purpose of helping these countries to repel aggression and strengthen their independence.

The threat to the free nations of southeast Asia has long been clear. The North Vietnamese regime has constantly sought to take over South Vietnam and Laos. This Communist regime has violated the Geneva accords for Vietnam. It has systematically conducted a campaign of subversion, which included the direction, training and supply of personnel and arms for the conduct of guerrilla warfare in South Vietnamese territory. In Laos, the North Vietnamese regime

has maintained military forces, used Laotian territory for infiltration into South Vietnam, and most recently carried out combat operations — all in direct violation of the Geneva agreements of 1962. ...

As President of the United States, I have concluded that I should now ask Congress, on its part, to join in affirming the national determination that all such attacks will be met, and that the United States will continue in the basic policy of assisting the free nations of the area to defend their freedom.

As I have repeatedly made clear, the United States intends no rashness, and seeks no wider war. We must make it clear to all that the United States is united in its determination to bring about the end of Communist subversion and aggression in the area. We seek the full and effective restoration of the international agreements signed in Geneva in 1954, with respect to South Vietnam, and again in Geneva in 1962, with respect to Laos. ...

I recommend a resolution expressing the support of the Congress for all necessary action to protect our Armed Forces and to assist nations covered by the SEATO Treaty. At the same time, I assure the Congress that we shall continue readily to explore any avenues of political solution that will effectively guarantee the removal of Communist subversion and the preservation of the independence of the nations of the area. ...

The events of this week would in any event have made the passage of a congressional resolution essential. But there is an additional reason for doing so at a time when we are entering on three months of political campaigning. Hostile nations must understand that in such a period the United States will continue to protect its national interests, and that in these matters there is no division among us. ...

Sources: National Archives and the Department of State Bulletin, August 24, 1964

Juan M. Ledesma (left) served in the Army Air Cavalry in Vietnam in 1965, and in October he fought at Ia Drang, the site of a battle re-created in the Mel Gibson film 'We Were Soldiers.'

Contributed p

Contributed photo

Sgt. Ramon Hernandez Torres served in Company A, 2nd Battalion, 39th Infantry, 9th Infantry Division in Vietnam. He was killed in action on Nov. 24, 1967.

Killed in Action

By Capt. Harold G. Minter

"On the afternoon of the 24th of November, Ramon was with his company on a search and destroy operation in Bien Hoa Province, Republic of Vietnam, when he was hit with enemy small arms fire. It may be of some comfort to know that death came quickly."

Contributed photo

Airman Second Class Xavier F. Gonzalez works at his last assignment in the Separations Section at Laughlin Air Force Base in Del Rio in April 1962. His tour began in 1957, and he served in North Africa, including Tripoli.

Jesus Gonzalez (left) and Juan Bautista pull guard duty in Vietnam in 1967. Both live in Corpus Christi.

Contributed by Juan S. Bautista

Spc. 5 Thomas E. Osbun is awarded the Air Medal abo
the USNS Corpus Christi Bay off the coast of South V
nam in 1967. Osbun served in the Army from 1965 to 19

Troops on patrol in September 1967.

Marine Sgt. John B. Large (right), 26, and a friend were
of a special unit stationed at Hoa Hiep, Vietnam, in 19
Their mission, aside from fighting enemy troops, wa
build a school and administer a public health program.

Contributed photo

Army Cpl. Emilio Rodela Jr., serving with B Battery in the 4th Infantry Division, sits on his seasonally decorated weaponry at Base Camp Bear Cat in South Vietnam. Rodela served in the Army from 1965 to 1967.

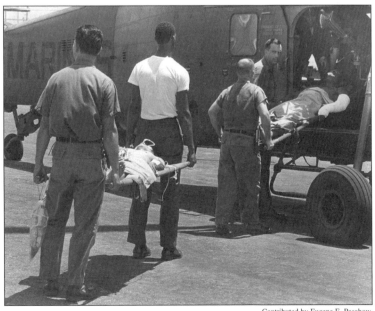

Eugene E. Pasahow (fourth from the left) assists wounded servicemen onto a transport in Da Nang, Vietnam, in October 1967.

Contributed by Eugene E. Pasahow

Contributed by Danny Flanag

Army Spc. John Daniel Flanagan, 21, travels in a convoy in Vietnam in June 1969. Flanagan served 14 months with U.S. Army, Pacific.

James Kaelin (left) with a friend in the Mekong Delta in Vietnam in 1968.

Contributed photo

Contributed photo

Army Cpl. Lonnie Joseph Ducote Jr. was killed in Binh Thuan, South Vietnam, in 1967.

Contributed photo

Air Force Capt. Lowell V. Thomas prepares for a mission in Saigon in 1965. He retired in 1984 as a lieutenant colonel.

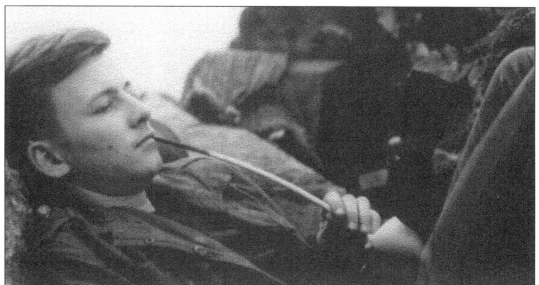

Contributed by Robert V. Poe Jr.

Robert V. Poe Jr., an Army soldier, reclines beside an M-60 tank in a field south of Munich, Germany, in 1968.

Caller-Times file

A helicopter picks up wounded soldiers in March 1966.

Contributed by Ovidio Garcia

my Spc. 4 Hector L. Garcia trains to become a paratrooper in Vietnam in 1968.

Contributed by Jerry K. Campbell

Major Jerry K. Campbell at Headquarters Building, 199th Light Infantry Brigade, at Long Binh Post, Vietnam, March 1968.

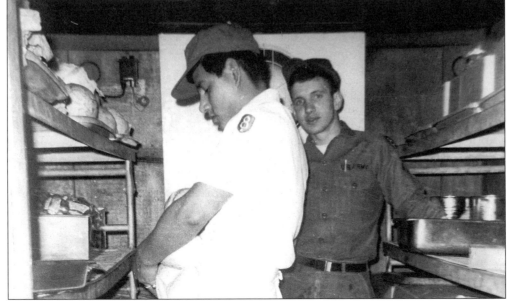

Contributed by Richard Guerrero Sr.

Army Staff Sgt. Richard Guerrero Sr. (left) in Baunholder, West Germany, in 1969.

Contributed by Craig R. Newberry

Craig Newberry took this picture of Marine Pfc. Dwight King Satterwhite in Quang Nam,
South Vietnam, in September 1966. A sniper killed Satterwhite a few days later.

Contributed by C.M. 'Skip' Henkel III

C.M. 'Skip' Henkel III in Saigon, South Vietnam, in 1970.

Contributed by Dolores Quintero

Francisco Garza in Vietnam.

Contributed by Eugene E. Pasahow

Bob Hope and Ann Margret entertain the troops in Cho Lai, Vietnam, in 1968.

National Archives

President Richard M. Nixon's Speech on Cambodia
April 30, 1970

Ten days ago, in my report to the Nation on Vietnam, I announced a decision to withdraw an additional 150,000 Americans from Vietnam over the next year. I said then that I was making that decision despite our concern over increased enemy activity in Laos, Cambodia, and in South Vietnam.

At that time, I warned that if I concluded that increased enemy activity in any of these areas endangered lives of Americans remaining in Vietnam, I would not hesitate to take strong and effective measures.

Despite that warning, North Vietnam has increased its military aggression in all these areas, and particularly in Cambodia.

After full consultation with the National Security Council, Ambassador Bunker, General Abrams, and my other advisors, I have concluded that the actions of the enemy in the last 10 days clearly endanger the lives of Americans who are in Vietnam now and would constitute an unacceptable risk to those who will be there after withdrawal of another 150,000.

To protect our men who are in Vietnam and to guarantee the continued success of our withdrawal and Vietnamization programs, I have concluded that the time has come for action.

Tonight, I shall describe the actions of the enemy, the actions I have ordered to deal with that situation, and the reasons for my decision. Cambodia, a small country of 7 million people, has been a neutral nation since the Geneva agreement of 1954, an agreement, incidentally, which was signed by the Government of North Vietnam.

American policy since then has been to scrupulously respect the neutrality of the Cambodian people. We have maintained a skeleton diplomatic mission of fewer than 15 in Cambodia's capital, and that only since last August. For the previous four years, from 1965 to 1969, we did not have any diplomatic mission whatever in Cambodia. And for the past four years, we have provided no military assistance whatever and no economic assistance to Cambodia.

North Vietnam, however, has not respected that neutrality. For the past four years as indicated on this map that you see here North Vietnam has occupied military sanctuaries all along the Cambodian frontier with South Vietnam. Some of these extend up to 20 miles into Cambodia.... In cooperation with the armed forces of South Vietnam, attacks are being launched this week to clean out major enemy sanctuaries on the Cambodian Vietnam border.

A major responsibility for the ground operations is being assumed by South Vietnamese forces. ...

There is one area, however, immediately above Parrot's Beak, where I have concluded that a combined American and South Vietnamese operation is necessary.

Reynaldo Caceres aims his weapon in Vietnam in 1970.

Contributed photo

Tonight, American and South Vietnamese units will attack the headquarters for the entire Communist military operation in South Vietnam. This key control center has been occupied by the North Vietnamese and Vietcong for five years in blatant violation of Cambodia's neutrality.

This is not an invasion of Cambodia. The areas in which these attacks will be launched are completely occupied and controlled by North Vietnamese forces. Our purpose is not to occupy the areas. Once enemy forces are driven out of these sanctuaries and once their military supplies are destroyed, we will withdraw....

We take this action not for the purpose of expanding the war into Cambodia but for the purpose of ending the war in Vietnam and winning the just peace we all desire. We have made and we will continue to make every possible effort to end this war through negotiation at the conference table rather than through more fighting on the battlefield. ...

The action that I have announced tonight puts the leaders of North Vietnam on notice that we will be patient in working for peace; we will be conciliatory at the conference table, but we will not be humiliated. We will not be defeated. We will not allow American men by the thousands to be killed by an enemy from privileged sanctuaries. ...

My fellow Americans, we live in an age of anarchy, both abroad and at home. We see mindless attacks on all the great institutions which have been created by free civilizations in the last 500 years. Even here in the United States, great universities are being systematically destroyed. ...

If, when the chips are down, the world's most powerful nation, the United States of America, acts like a pitiful, helpless giant, the forces of totalitarianism and anarchy will threaten free nations and free institutions throughout the world.

It is not our power but our will and character that is being tested tonight.... I have rejected all political considerations in making this decision. ...

Whether my party gains in November is nothing compared to the lives of 400,000 brave Americans fighting for our country and for the cause of peace and freedom in Vietnam. Whether I may be a one-term President is insignificant compared to whether by our failure to act in this crisis the United States proves itself to be unworthy to lead the forces of freedom in this critical period in world history.

I would rather be a one-term President and do what I believe is right than to be a two-term President at the cost of seeing America become a second rate power and to see this Nation accept the first defeat in its proud 190-year history. ...

Source: Public Papers of the Presidents of the United States: Richard Nixon, 1970, pp.405-409.

Jose Luis Sandoval mans his position at Fire Base Lawrence in Vietnam in June 1970.

Contributed photo

Contributed by Marc Cisnero

Marc Cisneros (seated) with his friends in Vietnam Christmas 1972. This was a picture made for a Christmas card they sent to their families.

Contributed by Royce D. Tate

Air Force Lt. Col. Royce D. Tate at Phan Rang Air Base, South Vietnam, in 1969.

Contributed by Dolores Quintero

Army Sgt. Albert Guajardo Jr. in Pleiku, Vietnam, in July 1971.

```
COMOUT      TSC    000    624 APR. 29,75 1612+     0441464000*****
4,COMOUT,011
FASTCAST



XXKK,ONEL
S̶E̶C̶R̶E̶T̶
  523-119-FYI (OT25) FREQUENT WIND (C)
  REPORTS ARE THAT THERE ARE 200 AMERICANS LEFT TO EVAC.
  GUNNER SIX TO GSF COMMANDER BRING UR PERSONNEL UP THRU
  TH BUILDING DO NOT LET THEM ( THE SOUTH VIETS) FOLLOW
  TOO CLOSELY.  USE MACE IF NECESSARY BUT DO NOT
  FIRE ON THEM.
  --2109Z


  CC98533
```

CLASSIFIED / CLASSIFIED

GERALD R FORD LIBRARY

Gerald R. Ford Presidential Library and Museum

A helicopter transmission during the evacuation of Saigon, April 29, 1975.

Gerald R. Ford Presidential Library and Museum

Secretary of State Henry Kissinger (from left), Vice President Nelson Rock-
efeller and President Gerald R. Ford discuss the evacuation of Saigon in
Washington, D.C., on April 28, 1975.

Corpus Christi Caller

92nd Year—No. 100 CORPUS CHRISTI, TEXAS, WEDNESDAY, APRIL 30, 1975 Want Ads 882-5401 Other Depts. 884-2011 56 Pages—Price 15 cents

South Vietnam surrenders to Viet Cong

SAIGON (AP) — South Vietnam declared unconditional surrender to the Viet Cong Wednesday, ending 30 years of warfare.

President Duong Van "Big" Minh spoke to the nation only hours after an armada of U.S. Marine helicopters had completed an emergency evacuation of nearly 900 Americans and thousands of Vietnamese from the besieged capital.

Minh, a retired general and neutralist, was named president Monday in a desperate and unsuccessful attempt to negotiate a peace with the Communist leaders.

In a five-minute radio address, Minh said "The Republic of Vietnam policy is the policy of peace and reconciliation, aimed at saving the blood of our people. I ask all servicemen to stop firing and stay where you are. I also demand that soldiers of the Provisional Revolutionary Government (Viet Cong) stop firing and stay in place.

Related stories and picture are on page 2A

"We are here waiting for the Provisional Revolutionary Government, to hand over authority in order to stop useless bloodshed."

Gen. Nguyen Huu Hanh, deputy chief of staff, then went on the air to order all South Vietnamese troops to carry out Minh's orders. "All commanders must be ready to enter into relations with commanders of the Provisional Revolutionary Government to carry out the cease-fire without bloodshed," he said.

As they spoke, Saigon fell silent and shellfire subsided along the northern rim where Viet Cong gunners had been bombarding the airport.

Saigon police and militiamen remained at their posts, indicating the Communist-led troops had not yet entered the city.

Some South Vietnamese officers complained that the evacuation of Americans had caused panic in the military, with many top army officers and most of the air force fleeing.

But it had been obvious that the capital would fall. More than a dozen North Vietnamese-Viet Cong divisions were ringing Saigon, which was defended by less than one division of demoralized green troops.

Associated Press special correspondent Peter Arnett, touring the city, reported nervous soldiers fired occasionally into the air but he saw no dead or wounded. Soldiers near the radio station at the northeastern edge of town said Communist-led forces had moved up to the Saigon River bridge and were poised to enter the city.

Streets around the abandoned U.S Embassy and ambassador's residence were littered with papers and broken

See Fighting, page 12A

PRESIDENT FORD
... 'close ranks'

Evacuation complete

6,000 Americans, 56,000 South Vietnamese taken out

WASHINGTON (AP) — The United States completed the month-long evacuation of more than 6,000 Americans and about 56,000 South Vietnamese from Saigon on Tuesday as President Ford called on the nation "to close ranks, to avoid recrimination about the past."

When word was flashed to the White House that Ambassador Graham Martin and the last evacuees had been airlifted from South Vietnam, Ford declared: "This action closes a chapter in the American experience."

Some 6,500 were rescued on the last day, about 1,000 of them Americans. Ford said it was now time "to look ahead to the many goals we share and to work together on the great tasks that remain to be accomplished."

Delays blamed on bad weather, pilot fatigue and difficult helicopter landings stretched out the day's withdrawal, which marked the end of U.S. involvement in the Vietnam war — a war that Secretary of State Henry A. Kissinger acknowledged did not meet U.S. objectives.

But, sharing the President's sentiments, Kissinger said, "It is a time to heal wounds, to look to our international obligations and to remember that peace and progress in the world have depended importantly on American commitment and American conviction..."

Two U.S. marine pilots were lost in the final effort when their helicopter fell into the South China Sea.

White House Press Secretary Ron Nessen said the operation was extended several hours because "a lot more Vietnamese were taken out than had been planned."

He said other reasons were occasional bad weather and pilot weariness. In addition, only two helicopters could go in at one time to make pickups from the embassy roof and the parking lot, he said.

In a briefing, Secretary of State Henry A. Kissinger rejected suggestions that Ambassador Martin resisted this last withdrawal. "He was in a very difficult position," Kissinger said, "he felt a moral obligation to the people with whom he was associated."

"He attempted to save as many people as possible. That's not the worst fault a man can have."

Kissinger said the United States moved deliberately over the last few weeks to avoid panic among the local population and to save many of the 5,000 to 8,000 South Vietnamese thought to be in a "high risk"

See Ford, page 12A

HENRY KISSINGER
... 'time to heal wound'

Congress turns to refugees as events outrace aid bill

WASHINGTON (AP) — With Americans already evacuated from South Vietnam, Congress appeared ready Tuesday night to scrap a $327-million aid bill authorizing U.S. evacuation forces and start over on a new bill.

House International Relations Chairman Thomas E. Morgan, D-Pa., said he thinks a new bill authorizing only funds for Cambodian and South Vietnamese refugees might "be a lot more than $327 million."

House Speaker Carl Albert said he agreed with Morgan that Congress should start over on a new bill rather than try to fix the old one.

Morgan said he thinks the cost will be higher to cover evacuation costs which the military already has incurred plus new costs for bringing refugees to the United States and housing them at three military bases.

Albert had ordered the $327 million humanitarian aid bill — with the authority for Ford to use U.S. military forces in the evacuation — pulled off the House floor just after preliminary work on it began.

Albert telephoned the order from the White House, where he said Ford had agreed during a meeting with congressional leaders that he no longer needed the authority in the bill.

While proposing a new bill, Morgan harshly criticized Albert for pulling the old bill off the House floor.

He said Congress should have acted before the evacuation was over to assert the principle that use of U.S. troops in hostilities abroad must be authorized by Congress.

Morgan said Congress has been trying to make clear since 1973 that the president may use military forces in hostilities abroad "only when authorized to do so by the Congress. We are now being told to retreat from that principle."

But Morgan said he will now consult with members of the Senate Foreign Relations Committee on starting from scratch on a new bill to provide U.S. aid to Cambodian as well as South Vietnamese refugees.

"Our committee ought to meet and find out exactly how many people have been evacuated, where to, and what costs have been incurred," Morgan said in a written statement. "Then and only then can the Congress make a sensible and responsible decision on how those costs should be met."

Two killed, 50 burned in truck blast

EAGLE PASS (AP) — A butane gas truck exploded here Tuesday afternoon killing at least two people, and injuring about 50. At least two other persons were reported missing, including the driver of the truck.

Twenty-one of the injured, many with burns over 80 per cent of their bodies, were taken to the Burns Center at Brooke Army Medical Center in San Antonio. The truck, owned by Surtigas, a company from Piedras Negras, a Mexican city across the border from Eagle Pass, split in two as it tried to avoid hitting a car and overturned and exploded, police said.

The truck erupted into a ball of flame that shot up about 200 feet in the air. One half of the truck rocketed into a mobile home park about 400 yards away and hit three homes.

"We have two dead at the hospital. One was dead on arrival," said Ruben Fernandez, administrator of the Eagle Pass Hospital.

Fernandez said at least 17 of those injured were in critical condition. A team of burns experts from the military installation rushed to Eagle Pass.

Fernandez said late Tuesday 42 persons were still in the hospital.

A spokesman for the Sheriff's office said the driver of the truck, identified as Jesus Verduzco, was still missing. So was the driver of a car that was immediately in front of the truck when the explosion occurred.

The spokesman said the truck apparently tried to avoid a collision in front of a used car lot and junk yard and overturned and exploded.

One half of the truck landed in the car lot spitting fire over cars and setting gas tanks on fire.

"There were many explosions," said Andrew McBeath. "There were a lot of people in the car lot which is also a repair shop. The place just caught on fire. There was fire on both sides of the highway."

McBeath said drivers of other cars on the highway tried to stop as the fire rushed towards them. "They jumped out of their cars and some of the cars just kept on going and caught on fire."

Twister kills three in Medina County

YANCEY (AP) — A tornado sucked a young girl out of her mother's arms and killed two other people and injured five in this small South Central Texas community.

The twister, which roared in from the east cutting a path eight miles long and about half mile wide, destroyed seven homes and damaged at least nine more. It uprooted trees and knocked out electric power.

The Department of Public Safety identified the dead as Dotty Moncada, 2, and Mr. and Mrs. Ernest Wielmers. Their ages were not given.

Earlier in the day thunderstorms and large hail had hit the Medina County area.

The tornado first hit the farm property of E. D. Dubois about three miles from the town. "It missed my house by a few yards," he said. "It went right through one of my pastures going east, then it went back up."

The first house destroyed resulted in the death of Dotty Moncada. A rescuer said Mrs. Moncada was in the house holding her children when the tornado struck. "She had both children in her arms," he said. "The tornado sucked one of them (Dotty) out of her arms as some appliances fell on Mrs. Moncada."

The girl's body was found about 600 yards from the house.

Mrs. Moncada and her older daughter were in fair condition at the county hospital late Tuesday. Mrs. Moncada suffered a fractured pelvis, fractured arm and lacerations.

Ambulances and rescue teams from Hondo were sent to Yancey shortly after the tornado hit at about 3:30 p.m.

Meanwhile in Central Texas, tornadoes were reported on the ground in Milam County, but no injuries or damage were reported.

Thunderstorms ranged throughout North Central Texas and Northeast Texas with warnings issued throughout the afternoon and early evening.

The National Weather Service said that large hail would accompany some of the thunderstorms.

West Texas was mostly under sunny skies following a cold front that began to dissipate early in the day.

The Weather Service said fair skies should prevail in West Texas Wednesday while cloudy to partly cloudy skies with showers and thundershowers were expected over the rest of the state.

Elsewhere in the nation, spring continued its fickle ways with so much snow and cold that stockmen's alerts were issued in parts of Wyoming and Montana.

Rain showers and some snow showers were scattered from the Rockies to the Great Lakes region. Rain patterns also appeared along the central Atlantic Coast and from the Mississippi Valley to the coasts of Georgia and South Carolina.

The northern Black Hills city of Lead, S.D., was crippled by 14 inches of new snow in 24 hours.

Del Mar regents rescind pay raise to avoid penalty

By MARY ALICE DAVIS
Staff Writer

Choosing to switch rather than fight with the keepers of the legislative pursestrings, the Del Mar College board of regents yesterday rescinded an employe pay raise approved last month.

Dr. Jean Richardson, college president, said he was reluctantly recommending the action in an effort to mend fences with the House Appropriations Committee. The committee last week decided to penalize junior colleges which granted mid-year pay hikes.

Richardson said the college staff was disappointed but understood the need to rescind the pay raise. He said he hoped the board would more than make up the loss when setting salaries at budget time this summer.

Richardsen said Del Mar apparently got caught in the fire from some influential legislator who seemed to think the junior colleges had "ripped them off" for $18 million and were bent on vengeance.

The $18 million was sent to Texas junior colleges as an emergency - aid appropriation. Richardson said the money was to compensate for under-funding in the past two years because of bigger-than-anticipated enrollment increases. There was no prohibition against spending it on salaries, he added.

But the House committee agreed that junior colleges using any of the money for pay hikes would have their appropriation cut by an equal amount for each of the next two years. Four colleges were named.

Related story, page 1B

Del Mar's raise would have cost $250,000 to $300,000. The college stood to lose $500,000 to $600,000 in state aid over two years if the committee action was accepted by the Legislature.

Richardson said there was a chance the committee decision could be overridden but that he didn't want to "gamble" on it. There is "a lot of frenzy and furor" in the closing month of a session, he said.

"The odds don't appear very attractive," Richardson told the board.

He suggested using the money previously earmarked for the raises to buy equipment and supplies which otherwise would have been paid for out of next year's budget. This would free local tax money for pay raises in next year's budget, he said.

He said he hoped the board would make up for loss of the midyear raise plus grant a regular first - of - the - year increase this summer.

Regent William Shireman Sr. said the board would have to be careful about creating a "Frankenstein situation," apparently referring to the possibility of setting a precedent with an extra-large raise.

The mid-year raise amounted to about 7 per cent on an annual basis but covered only January to August. It had been authorized but not granted since the college had not received all the money.

The regents voted 5-1 to accept Richardson's recommendation. Dr. Clotilde Garcia cast the "no" vote. Absent from the one-issue special meeting were Fred Heldenfels and Jose Montoya. The nine-member board currently has one vacancy.

Dr. Garcia had inquired about the possibility of a lobbying effort to head off the committee plan.

Richardson said junior colleges had not misled the Legislature to get the emergency funds by billing the need as urgent. One junior college, Texarkana, did say it couldn't make it through the year without help, then used some of its money for a pay raise, Richardson said, indicating that this may have started the trouble.

See Del Mar, page 12A

Weather

Corpus Christi and vicinity will have partly cloudy skies and continued warm weather today and tomorrow. There is a 20 per cent chance of showers or thundershowers today. High temperatures today and tomorrow will be near 90, with an overnight low in the middle 70s. Winds will be southeasterly 10 to 20 miles an hour today; gusty near heavier showers.

Index

Rep. Newton front runner for FPC spot

State Rep. Jon Newton of Beeville reportedly is in line for appointment to the Federal Power Commission.

Announcement of an appointment to the agency will come from the White House and must have the consent of the Senate Commerce Committee.

Sen. John Tower of Texas reportedly recommended Newton to the White House and Sen. Lloyd M. Bentsen "does not object" to Newton.

The Federal Power Commission is empowered to regulate interstate gas pipelines and sets the price of natural gas at the wellhead. Now under consideration is legislation to authorize the FPC to regulate the price of intrastate gas.

In light of the energy crisis, the FPC has increased in importance in recent months.

Sen. Max Sherman of Amarillo apparently was at one time a prime candidate for the FPC appointment, along with Newton and several others, but the field reportedly has narrowed to Newton.

High absentee vote signals interest in coming election

A record 1,400 persons voted absentee in person for Saturday's election before the deadline yesterday.

City Secretary Bill Read said the absentee vote indicates a record total vote "in the neighborhood of 40,000 votes."

Long lines waited at City Hall all day yesterday as 535 persons cast ballots. This vote alone was greater than the total absentee voting in the May general election two years ago.

Read said he mailed out 49 ballots to persons unable to vote in person. These must be returned by 1 p.m. Saturday.

The record high vote stands at 36,650 in the May 1, 1971, election. At that time there were 984 absentee votes.

In the May 5, 1973, election, there were 522 absentee ballots and a total vote of 14,246. In the May 22, 1973, runoff election there were 808 absentee votes and a total of 41,049.

Last Jan. 18 a special election drew 858 absentee and 25,089 votes.

LAST DAY OF ABSENTEE VOTING DRAWS CROWD AT CITY HALL

Caller-Times archives

Comedian Jonathan Winters autographed a cast and later autographed the photo of the event. He wrote, "To Sargent Pina — You're a 'special guy' in a special outfit. Semper Fi, Jonathan Winters."

Contributed by Roberto Pina

Army Reserve Lt. Col. Xavier Montalvo served in Panama from 1990 to 1991, following the U.S. invasion of the Central American nation in 1989 to capture dictator Gen. Manuel Noriega.

Contributed by Gracie Garcia

Contributed by Sara

Bob Hope entertains the multinational peacekeeping fo in Beirut for Christmas 1983.

A New World:

Sept. 11, 2001, Afghanistan and Iraq

A New World Timeline

Hussein

George H.W. Bush

Schwarzkopf

Clinton

Rumsfeld

George W. Bush

1990

Iraqi dictator **SADDAM HUSSEIN** directs the invasion of Kuwait.

U.S. president GEORGE H.W. BUSH vows that Saddam's actions "will not stand."

U.S. forces arrive in Saudi Arabia. Operation Desert Shield begins.

United Nations resolution directs the removal of Iraqis from Kuwait.

1991

Congress authorizes President Bush to remove Iraq from Kuwait with military force. The operations will be led by **Central Command commander Gen. H. NORMAN SCHWARZKOPF.**

Jan. 15, the U.N. deadline for Iraqi withdrawal, is ignored in Iraq. The Allied air campaign against Iraq begins the next day.

Operation Desert Storm, the coalition attack on Iraqi forces in Kuwait, begins. Iraq agrees to a cease-fire 100 hours later.

The Bush administration limits its action to the confines of the U.N. resolution and does not move to depose Saddam Hussein or stop him from repressing the emboldened Kurdish and Shi'ite opposition.

U.N. passes Resolution 687, ordering Hussein to destroy all weapons of mass destruction or face enduring economic sanctions.

1992

U.S. economic problems engulf President Bush, and **BILL CLINTON** defeats him for the presidency.

1998

DONALD RUMSFELD is among a number of critics calling on Clinton to stop Iraqi WMD production.

Iraq refuses to cooperate with U.N. weapons inspectors. As he faces impeachment, Clinton orders four days of air strikes on Iraq.

2000

Texas Gov. **GEORGE W. BUSH** narrowly defeats Vice President Al Gore for the presidency. He appoints Rumsfeld defense secretary and Gen. Colin Powell secretary of state.

2001

Al-Qaeda terrorists fly airliners into the World Trade Center and the Pentagon, and a fourth plane crashes in Pennsylvania. Three thousand people are killed.

Bin Laden

Powell

Bush in flight suit

Sanchez

OSAMA BIN LADEN, the leader of the al-Qaeda terrorist group, is accused of masterminding the Sept. 11 attacks.

Bush establishes a new Office of Homeland Security and selects Pennsylvania Gov. Tom Ridge to lead it.

Bush directs war planners to prepare operations against the Taliban, who harbor al Qaeda operatives, in Afghanistan and against Hussein in Iraq.

Operation Enduring Freedom, the U.S. invasion of Afghanistan, begins.

2002

Bush calls Iraq, North Korea and Iran an "axis of evil."

Congress approves the use of military for against Iraq.

The United Nations passes Resolution 144 to begin weapons inspections in Iraq. Iraq refuses to cooperate with inspector

The Department of Homeland Security is established.

2003

U.S. troops move to the Persian Gulf.

France announces that it will oppose any move to begin a war in Iraq.

Secretary of State COLIN POWELL argues the Bush administration's case before the U.N. Security Council, to little effect.

The British try one last time through diplomatic channels to defuse the situation, and 200,000 U.S. troops and five carrie groups converge on the Middle East.

Bush issues 48-hour ultimatum to Hussein ordering him to leave Iraq.

Hussein refuses to leave Iraq. U.S. forces attack Iraqi installations, and Operation Iraqi Freedom begins.

As British forces take Basra, U.S. forces race northward, bypassing Iraqi cities and drive toward Baghdad.

Baghdad is surrounded, and U.S. tanks probe freely into the city.

Iraqi civilians loot Baghdad, and U.S. troops help them pull down a statue of Hussein

Aboard the USS Lincoln, **President Bush announces the end of the war** in Iraq.

Rio Grande City native **Lt. Gen. RICARDO SANCHEZ** assumes command of U.S. forces in Iraq.

Uday and Qusay Hussein, sons of Saddam are killed in Iraq during a U.S. raid.

Insurgents attack occupation forces with rocket-propelled grenades and bombs.

Sources: PBS.org, the U.S. State Department, the U.S. Hou Representatives, the White House, the Defense Department the George Bush Presidential Library and Museum

Thursday

FORECAST
Mostly Cloudy
30% chance of rain
High 68, low 52.   B2

SPECIAL REPORT
War in the Persian Gulf

INSIDE
15 pages of
coverage

Corpus Christi Caller-Times

Copyright © 1991 Caller-Times Publishing Company

35 Cents | More than 167,000 daily readers | January 17, 1991

'The world could wait no longer'

Allies attack

Massive air strikes target nuclear, chemical, war facilities

At a Glance: War in the Persian Gulf

The United States and its allies went to war against Iraq as hundreds of warplanes unleashed a massive bombing attack./A1

Commanders of the air armada that attacked Iraq hope to sow panic among Iraqi troops, but ground commanders still expect bitter infantry battles./A6

WORLD:
American students attending college in Jerusalem were unfazed by the attack. One said, it's safer here than walking the streets of New York./B4

LOCAL:
A 19-year-old Corpus Christi resident and sophomore at the University of Texas in Austin returned to the United States early Wednesday after spending seven days with a peace delegation in Jordan and Iraq./B4

Two South Texas lawmakers, watching war being waged via national television, held contrasting viewpoints about Bush's decision to bomb Baghdad. U.S. Rep. Solomon Ortiz supported Bush but state Sen. Carlos Truan opposed the war./B4

About 80 relatives of soldiers gathered in the basement of the Corpus Cathedral for prayer, song and support./B4

BUSINESS:
Some oil companies responded to the war with Iraq by immediately freezing their wholesale price of gasoline./C7

Dozens of U.S. companies, including many in Texas and at least one in Corpus Christi, have been contacted by an official of the Kuwait Recovery Program about helping in restoration of the country./C8

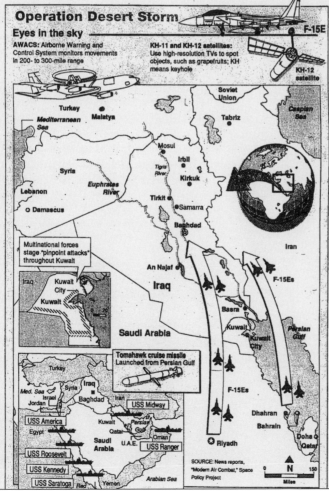

Operation Desert Storm

Eyes in the sky

AWACS: Airborne Warning and Control System monitors movements in 200- to 300-mile range

KH-11 and KH-12 satellites: Use high-resolution TVs to spot objects, such as grapefruits; KH means keyhole

F-15E

KH-12 satellite

Multinational forces stage "pinpoint attacks" throughout Kuwait

Tomahawk cruise missile launched from Persian Gulf

SOURCE: News reports, "Modern Air Combat," Space Policy Project

Bush: 'The battle has been joined': Iraqis apparently caught unprepared

By Rick Atkinson
And David S. Broder
THE WASHINGTON POST

The United States and its allies went to war against Iraq Wednesday night as hundreds of warplanes unleashed a massive bombing attack against targets in Iraq and occupied Kuwait.

"Tonight the battle has been joined," President Bush said in a brief, nationally televised address at 8 p.m. CST. "Our goal is not the conquest of Iraq, it is the liberation of Kuwait."

Wave after wave of warplanes attacked Baghdad, hitting oil refineries, the international airport and the presidential palace of President Saddam Hussein. Witnesses reported the night sky was thick with tracer fire from antiaircraft guns and a smoky pallor had settled over the Iraqi capital. Western correspondents reported much of the city had been blacked out, although not until nearly an hour after the raids began.

The first targets hit, according to U.S. military sources in Saudi Arabia, were ground-to-ground Scud missiles capable of striking Saudi or Israeli cities. "Our planes

President Bush: 'Our goal is not the conquest of Iraq, it is the liberation of Kuwait.'

went in. The bombs went down. There has been no reaction from the Iraqi side," said a Saudi spokesman in Dhahran.

Bush said the attacks also are intended to destroy Iraq's nuclear weapons potential and chemical weapons stocks, as well as damaging Saddam's tank force. "We will not fail," the president added.

The order to launch attacks
Please see **Attack**/A8

Congress closes ranks as nation goes to war

Lawmakers express support of U.S. troops

By John E. Yang
THE WASHINGTON POST

WASHINGTON — Members of Congress closed ranks Wednesday night to back the men and women waging a war many lawmakers had sought to avert four days earlier.

Even those who had strongly opposed giving President Bush the authorization he sought to launch Wednesday night's assault expressed their support for the soldiers, sailors, Marines and airmen engaged in Operation Desert Storm.

there be," said Sen. John Glenn, D-Ohio.

"We must now stand united in support of our armed forces in the gulf who have embraced the duty and burden of conducting the war," House Speaker Thomas S. Foley, D-Wash., said in a statement. "We must now pray for a conflict that ends quickly, decisively and with a minimum loss of life."

Texas congressmen said Wednesday they firmly supported Bush's decision to use force for what he described as "the libera-

Caller-Times archives

National Archives

President George H.W. Bush announces military action against Iraq
Jan. 16, 1991

Just 2 hours ago, allied air forces began an attack on military targets in Iraq and Kuwait. These attacks continue as I speak. Ground forces are not engaged. This conflict started August 2nd when the dictator of Iraq invaded a small and helpless neighbor. Kuwait — a member of the Arab League and a member of the United Nations — was crushed; its people, brutalized. Five months ago, Saddam Hussein started this cruel war against Kuwait. Tonight, the battle has been joined.

This military action, taken in accord with United Nations resolutions and with the consent of the United States Congress, follows months of constant and virtually endless diplomatic activity on the part of the United Nations, the United States, and many, many other countries. Arab leaders sought what became known as an Arab solution, only to conclude that Saddam Hussein was unwilling to leave Kuwait. Others traveled to Baghdad in a variety of efforts to restore peace and justice. Our Secretary of State, James Baker, held an historic meeting in Geneva, only to be totally rebuffed. ...

Now the 28 countries with forces in the Gulf area have exhausted all reasonable efforts to reach a peaceful resolution — have no choice but to drive Saddam from Kuwait by force. We will not fail.

As I report to you, air attacks are underway against military targets in Iraq. We are determined to knock out Saddam Hussein's nuclear bomb potential. We will also destroy his chemical weapons facilities.

Much of Saddam's artillery and tanks will be destroyed. Our operations are designed to best protect the lives of all the coalition forces by targeting Saddam's vast military arsenal. Initial reports from (Allied commander-in-chief Gen. Norman) Schwarzkopf are that our operations are proceeding according to plan.

Our objectives are clear: Saddam Hussein's forces will leave Kuwait. The legitimate government of Kuwait will be restored to its rightful place, and Kuwait will once again be free. Iraq will eventually comply with all relevant United Nations resolutions, and then, when peace is restored, it is our hope that Iraq will live as a peaceful and cooperative member of the family of nations, thus enhancing the security and stability of the Gulf. ...

Saddam was warned over and over again to comply with the will of the United Nations: Leave Kuwait, or be driven out. Saddam has arrogantly rejected all warnings. Instead, he tried to make this a dispute between Iraq and the United States of America.

Caller-Times file

Andy Alaniz, a 1989 graduate of Moody High School, was killed in Iraq in 1991, within hours of the cease-fire of hostilities.

Well, he failed. Tonight, 28 nations — countries from 5 continents, Europe and Asia, Africa, and the Arab League — have forces in the Gulf area standing shoulder to shoulder against Saddam Hussein. These countries had hoped the use of force could be avoided. Regrettably, we now believe that only force will make him leave.

Prior to ordering our forces into battle, I instructed our military commanders to take every necessary step to prevail as quickly as possible, and with the greatest degree of protection possible for American and allied service men and women. I've told the American people before that this will not be another Vietnam, and I repeat this here tonight. ...

We have no argument with the people of Iraq. Indeed, for the innocents caught in this conflict, I pray for their safety. Our goal is not the conquest of Iraq. It is the liberation of Kuwait. It is my hope that somehow the Iraqi people can, even now, convince their dictator that he must lay down his arms, leave Kuwait, and let Iraq itself rejoin the family of peace-loving nations. ...

Listen to Hollywood Huddleston, Marine lance corporal. He says, "Let's free these people, so we can go home and be free again." And he's right. The terrible crimes and tortures committed by Saddam's henchmen against the innocent peo-

ple of Kuwait are an affront to mankind and a challenge to the freedom of all.

Listen to one of our great officers out there, Marine Lieutenant General Walter Boomer. He said: "There are things worth fighting for. A world in which brutality and lawlessness are allowed to go unchecked isn't the kind of world we're going to want to live in."

Listen to Master Sergeant J.P. Kendall of the 82d Airborne: "We're here for more than just the price of a gallon of gas. What we're doing is going to chart the future of the world for the next 100 years. It's better to deal with this guy now than 5 years from now."

And finally, we should all sit up and listen to Jackie Jones, an Army lieutenant, when she says, "If we let him get away with this, who knows what's going to be next?"

Tonight, as our forces fight, they and their families are in our prayers. May God bless each and every one of them, and the coalition forces at our side in the Gulf, and may He continue to bless our nation, the United States of America.

Source: George Bush Presidential Library and Museum

Contributed photo

Albert Anthony Salazar (left) with his friend Christian in a helicopter during Operation Desert Storm in 1991.

Master Gunnery Sgt. Jose A. Gongora in Dubai during the Persian Gulf War. The Marine served from 1965 to 1995.

Contributed by Mr. and Mrs. D.C. Lujan

Col. Gregory Nelson Maisel and his Cobra attack helicopter in Saudi Arabia during Operation Desert Storm.

Contributed by Sara Maisel

Contributed by Maria Mireles

Senior Airman Xavier Paul Mireles (left) wears his gas mask in Saudi Arabia in 1991.

Contributed by Xavier Paul Mireles

Bob Hope visits the troops in Saudia Arabia in 1991.

Contributed photo

Ramiro Alejos Jr. with a Kuwaiti man and his herd of camels in March 1991.

Contributed by Dolores Quintero

Dennis R. Quintero (second from left), U.S. Air Force, squats in a tent with friends as they celebrate Mardi Gras during Operation Desert Storm in 1991.

Ramiro Alejos Jr. in northern Kuwait oilfields in March 1991.

Contributed photo

Contributed photo

Ramiro Alejos Jr. stands beside an Iraqi oil trench in southern Kuwait in March 1991.

Contributed photo

Two generations of naval aviators from the Coastal Bend: Robstown's Capt. Juan M. Garcia Jr. at the commissioning ceremony of his son, Ensign Juan M. Garcia III, at Naval Air Station Pensacola, Fla., in October 1992.

Denise Garcia greets her husband, Navy Lt. Juan Garcia III, at Naval Air Station Barber's Point, Hawaii, in December 1996. He returned from a Persian Gulf deployment.

Contributed photo

Contributed by Benjamin Chavez

Army Cpl. Benjamin Chavez in Kuwait in November 1994, 'hooked up with Benz,' he writes. Cpl. Chavez served in the U.S. Army from 1992 to 1996. He was stationed in Saudi Arabia and Kuwait.

Contributed photo

y 1st Lt. Rose Guerrero in Iraq in 2000.

Navy Lt. Matthew Crockett Roberts on an aircraft carrier in the Persian Gulf in 1997. Roberts was selected HC-2 Pilot of the Year for 2000, and he also received the Navy Air Medal for rescuing 44 people during a hurricane. He served in the Navy from 1996 to 2003.

Contributed by Steve and Susie Roberts

EXTRA EXTRA EXTRA

Corpus Christi Caller·Times

 50 cents   Serving South Texas since 1883 ❑ Copyright © 2001 Corpus Christi Caller-Times   September 12, 2001

AMERICA UNDER ATTACK

Trade Centers leveled; Pentagon hit; airliners down

One of the towers of the World Trade Center in New York collapses in this image made from television Tuesday. Planes crashed into the upper floors of both World Trade Center towers minutes apart Tuesday.   AP Photo/ABC

7:45 a.m. CDT	8:03 a.m. CDT	8:35 a.m. CDT	9 a.m. CDT
First plane crash into World Trade Center	Second crash into World Trade Center	President Bush addresses nation	747 jumbo jet crashes near Pittsburgh

Airports closed, buildings evacuated, some airlines report missing planes

Terrorists attack where 50,000 people work

BY JERRY SCHWARTZ
AP National Writer

NEW YORK — In a horrific sequence of destruction, terrorists crashed two planes into the World Trade Center, and the twin 110-story towers collapsed Tuesday morning. Explosions also rocked the Pentagon and spread fear across the nation.

"I have a sense it's a horrendous number of lives lost," Mayor Rudolph Giuliani said. "I don't know yet. Right now we have to focus on saving as many lives as possible."

Authorities had been trying to evacuate those who work in the twin towers, but many were thought to have been trapped. About 50,000 people work at the Trade Center.

"This is perhaps the most audacious terrorist attack that's ever taken place in the world," said Chris Yates, an aviation expert at Jane's Transport in London. "It takes a logistics operation from the terror group involved that is second to none. Only a very small handful of terror groups is on that list. ... I would name at the top of the list Osama bin Laden."

President Bush ordered a full-scale investigation to "hunt down the folks who committed this act."

Within the hour, an aircraft crashed on a helicopter landing pad near the Pentagon, and the White House, the Pentagon and the Capitol were evacuated.

In Pennsylvania, a large plane, believed to be a Boeing 747, crashed about 80 miles southeast of Pittsburgh. The fate of those aboard was not immediately known and it was not clear if the crash was related to the disasters elsewhere.

Authorities went on alert from coast to coast, halting all air traffic, evacuating high-profile buildings and tightening security at strategic installations. The Situation Room at the White House was in full operation.

"Everyone was screaming, crying, running, cops, people, firefighters, everyone," said Mike Smith, a fire marshal. "It's like a war zone."

"I just saw the building I work in come down," said businessman Gabriel Ioan, shaking in shock outside City Hall, a cloud of smoke and ash from the World Trade Center behind him. "I just saw the top of Trade Two come down."

Nearby a crowd mobbed a man on a pay phone, screaming at him to get off the phone so that they could call relatives. Dust and dirt flew everywhere. Ash was 2 to 3 inches deep in places.

Please see ATTACK/2

caller.com
More than **3,000,000** page views per month

Latest news develoents at Caller.com

The first of two extra editions published on Sept. 11, 2001.

Caller-Times archives

8 pages of special coverage inside

Corpus Christi Caller Times

50 cents

Serving South Texas since 1883 ☐ Copyright © 2001 Corpus Christi Caller-Times

Monday, October 8, 2001 ★ ★

■ 50 Tomahawk missiles fired in strike

■ Bush: 'Peace and freedom will prevail'

■ Taliban: Afghan civilians were killed

U.S. launches attack

Airport security may get tighter

By Stephanie L. Jordan
and Venessa Santos-Garza
Caller-Times

While cars backed up at Corpus Christi International Airport for identification checks and questions from armed soldiers, city leaders gathered Sunday in the basement at City Hall to make sure residents can go about their lives feeling as safe as possible.

The U.S. Coast Guard continued to carefully monitor ships at the Port of Corpus Christi, one of the Coastal Bend's largest employers and economic lifelines.

"The worst thing that can happen is to hunker down and have a bunker mentality and we're not going to let that happen," Mayor Loyd Neal said. "We have no reason to be concerned about anything, but we are prepared should anything happen."

The Emergency Operations Center at City Hall was up and running at 12:15 p.m., less than an hour after the start of attacks on Afghanistan. The center contained representatives from law enforcement agencies, the city, the port, the Coast Guard and city and refinery fire departments.

"Our two primary missions are to protect the community and to reassure (residents) to go about their daily routines," City Manager David Garcia said.

Added security

But some routines changed somewhat Sunday, most noticeably at the airport. And more changes at the airport could be in store today, officials said.

"This is the same stage of security we have had in al

Bombs, missiles strike Taliban

By Christopher S. Wren
and Jacques Steinberg
New York Times News Service

The United States, supported by Britain, launched its long-anticipated attack on Afghanistan on Sunday, dropping bombs and firing volleys of cruise missiles against Taliban military and communications facilities and suspected terrorist training bases.

The armada included 15 long-range bombers, 15 carrier-based jets and 50 Tomahawk missiles fired from American and British submarines, the Pentagon said.

The military phase of the campaign — begun just before noon Central time (9.5 hours later in Afghanistan) — started with the firing of 50 cruise missiles from British cruisers and submarines.

The missiles soon were followed with strikes by 15 land-based bombers and 25 F-14 and F-18 jets from the carriers Carl Vinson and Enterprise, dropping precision-guided bombs as well as more conventional explosives in wave after wave of thunderous barrages, according to Defense Secretary Donald Rumsfeld and Gen. Richard Myers, the chairman of the Joint Chiefs of Staff.

"Operations continue as we speak," Rumsfeld said at a briefing in Washington Sunday afternoon. Taliban air defenses and suspected terrorist training centers were among the main targets.

"They will be dust," one senior military official said of the training camps.

Military officials said the operation presaged at least a week of punishing airstrikes against Taliban posts, and that some missions might be carried out in daylight. "If we've done our job with their air defenses, there's no rea-

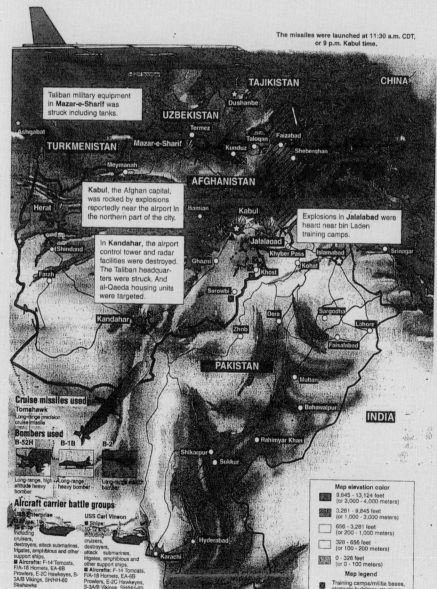

The missiles were launched at 11:30 a.m. CDT, or 9 p.m. Kabul time.

Taliban military equipment in **Mazar-e-Sharif** was struck including tanks.

Kabul, the Afghan capital, was rocked by explosions reportedly near the airport in the northern part of the city.

In **Kandahar**, the airport control tower and radar facilities were destroyed. The Taliban headquarters were struck. And al-Qaeda housing units were targeted.

Explosions in **Jalalabad** were heard near bin Laden training camps.

Cruise missiles used

Tomahawk
Long-range precision cruise missile

Bombers used

B-52H   B-1B   B-2

Long-range, high
altitude heavy
bomber

Long-range
heavy bomber

Long-range stealth
bomber

Aircraft carrier battle groups

USS Enterprise
■ Ships:
10-12 ships
including
cruisers,
destroyers, attack submarines,
frigates, amphibious and other
support ships.
■ Aircraft: F-14 Tomcats,
F/A-18 Hornets, EA-6B
Prowlers, E-2C Hawkeyes, S-
3A/B Vikings, SH/HH-60
Seahawks

USS Carl Vinson
■ Ships:
10-12 ships
including
cruisers,
destroyers,
attack submarines,
amphibious and
other support ships.
■ Aircraft: F-14 Tomcats,
F/A-18 Hornets, EA-6B
Prowlers, E-2C Hawkeyes,
S-3A/B Vikings, SH/HH-60

Map elevation color

| 9,845 - 13,124 feet (or 3,000 - 4,000 meters) |
| 3,281 - 9,845 feet (or 1,000 - 3,000 meters) |
| 656 - 3,281 feet (or 200 - 1,000 meters) |
| 328 - 655 feet (or 100 - 200 meters) |
| 0 - 328 feet (or 0 - 100 meters) |

Map legend
Training camps/militia bases,

Corpus Christi Caller Times

50 cents

More than 211,295 daily readers
Serving South Texas since 1883 □ Copyright © 2003 Corpus Christi Caller-Times

Thursday, March 20, 2003 • City edition ★★

War at dawn

Saddam on TV

He said the United States committed a "shameful crime" and urged his country to "draw your sword."

17 Iraqis give up

As many as 17 Iraqi soldiers surrendered to coalition forces along the Kuwaiti border.

Air raid sirens were heard in Baghdad on Thursday morning (around 8:40 p.m. Wednesday in Corpus Christi) amid explosions. U.S. bombs struck the capital in an attack aimed at Iraqi leaders. *Associated Press*

Bombs, missiles fired at Iraqi leaders

By David Espo
Associated Press

The United States launched the opening salvo Wednesday night of a war to topple Saddam Hussein, firing cruise missiles and precision-guided bombs into Baghdad. U.S. officials said the Iraqi leader himself was among the targets.

"This will not be a campaign of half-measures and we will accept no outcome but victory," President Bush said in an Oval Office address shortly after explosions ricocheted through the pre-dawn light of the Iraqi capital.

Anti-aircraft tracer fire arced across the Baghdad sky as the American munitions bore in on their targets. A ball of fire shot skyward after one explosion.

Saddam appeared on state-run television a few hours after the attack. He said the United States had committed a "shameful crime" by attacking Iraq, and urged Iraqis to "draw your sword" against the enemy. He appeared unhurt, and wore a military uniform.

The missiles struck less than two hours after the expiration of Bush's deadline for Saddam to surrender power or face war.

Bush described the targets as being of "military importance," and one White House official said the attack was the result of fresh intelligence that prompted an earlier-than-planned opening strike.

Two officials knowledgeable about the operation said the Iraqi dictator was among the "leadership targets" that the strikes were aimed at.

It was clear from Bush's words — he called it the opening stages of a "broad and concerted campaign" — that the war to topple the Iraqi dictator and eliminate his weapons of mass destruc-

Please see **MILITARY/A8**

"A campaign on the harsh terrain of a nation as large as California could be longer and more difficult than some predict."
— President Bush

Allies should not dismiss Iraq force

Country's military is smaller than in '91, but can still cause casualties

By Lisa Hoffman
Scripps Howard News Service

Nearly a dozen years ago, at the dawn of the 1991 Persian Gulf War, the military forces of Iraqi strongman Saddam Hussein were the fourth-mightiest in the world.

But even with more than 1 million men, 6,000 tanks and 700 warplanes, that army crumbled in a matter of days after the allied onslaught rolled into Iraq.

That was then. This is now: Iraq's forces are an even paler shadow of their former anemic selves.

As a consequence of that devastating combat rout, plus four U.S. missile attacks since, a decade-long international arms embargo, and years of American strikes against Iraqi targets in two no-fly zones, the dictator's military is less than half the strength it was at its height. Some analysts say it is barely a third as capable.

Today, Iraq's arsenal includes maybe 2,200

Associated Press

Troops seek terrorists in Afghan raid

Thousands participate in biggest operation in year

Associated Press

BAGRAM, Afghanistan — About 1,000 U.S. troops launched a raid on villages in south-eastern Afghanistan Thursday, hunting for members of the al-Qaeda terrorist network in the biggest U.S. operation in just over a year, military officials said.

Helicopters ferried troops from the Army's 82nd Airborne Division to the remote, mountainous area as the hunt for Osama bin Laden and his terror network intensified, according to U.S. military officials in Washington.

Military officials in Afghanistan confirmed the operation was under way, but would provide no details.

"I do not have anything to say about the Kandahar operation at this time," said Col. Roger King, U.S. army spokesman at the U.S.

Caller-Times archives

The White House

President George W. Bush announces military action against Iraq

March 20, 2003

My fellow citizens, at this hour, American and coalition forces are in the early stages of military operations to disarm Iraq, to free its people and to defend the world from grave danger. On my orders, coalition forces have begun striking selected targets of military importance to undermine Saddam Hussein's ability to wage war. These are opening stages of what will be a broad and concerted campaign. More than 35 countries are giving crucial support ... to help with intelligence and logistics, to the deployment of combat units. Every nation in this coalition has chosen to bear the duty and share the honor of serving in our common defense.

To all the men and women of the United States Armed Forces now in the Middle East, the peace of a troubled world and the hopes of an oppressed people now depend on you. That trust is well placed. ... In this conflict, America faces an enemy who has no regard for conventions of war or rules of morality. Saddam Hussein has placed Iraqi troops and equipment in civilian areas, attempting to use innocent men, women and children as shields for his own military — a final atrocity against his people.

I want Americans and all the world to know that coalition forces will make every effort to spare innocent civilians from harm. A campaign on the harsh terrain of a nation as large as California could be longer and more difficult than some predict. And helping Iraqis achieve a united, stable and free country will require our sustained commitment.

We come to Iraq with respect for its citizens, for their great civilization and for the religious faiths they practice. We have no ambition in Iraq, except to remove a threat and restore control of that country to its own people.

I know that the families of our military are praying that all those who serve will return safely and soon. Millions of Americans are praying with you for the safety of your loved ones and for the protection of the innocent. For your sacrifice, you have the gratitude and respect of the American people. And you can know that our forces will be coming home as soon as their work is done.

Our nation enters this conflict reluctantly — yet, our purpose is sure. The people of the United States and our friends and allies will not live at the mercy of an outlaw regime that threatens the peace with weapons of mass murder. We will meet that threat now, with our Army, Air Force, Navy, Coast Guard and Marines, so that we do not have to meet it later with armies of fire fighters and police and doctors on the streets of our cities.

Now that conflict has come, the only way to limit its duration is to apply decisive force. And I assure you, this will not be a campaign of half measures, and we will accept no outcome but victory.

My fellow citizens, the dangers to our country and the world will be overcome. We will pass through this time of peril and carry on the work of peace. We will defend our freedom. We will bring freedom to others and we will prevail. May God bless our country and all who defend her.

Source: U.S. State Department

Contributed

Marines board a charter plane as they head for Iraq in 2003.

Contributed by Jaime Juarez

The wreckage of a tank was a common sight in Iraq following
the U.S. invasion of the Middle Eastern nation in 2003.

A fire blazes
in the desert in
Rumaliyah, Ira
in 2003.

Contributed by Jaime Juarez

Contributed by Alicia Callejo

Private First Class Richard Michael Rodriguez takes a moment to smile as he mans his position in a M2A2 Bradley tank during Operation Iraqi Free-dom in Iraq in 2003. Pfc. Rodriguez has served in the U.S. Army since June 2001.

Jaime Juarez, a communications chief in the U.S. Marine Corps, stands in front of a destroyed Iraqi artillery position in 2003. Juarez is part of Commu-nications Compa-ny, HQBN, 1st Marine Division from Camp Pendleton, Calif.

Contributed by Jaime Juarez

Contributed by Jaime Juarez

Former Marine Lt. Col. Oliver North speaks with soldiers in Iraq in 2003.

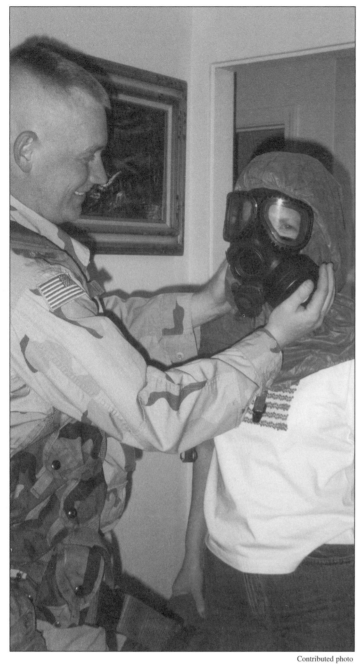

Contributed photo

Spc. 4 Casten John Mackerer shows his mother, Cindy Mackerer, how a gas masks feels in April 2003. Mackerer was shipping out for Iraq.

Contributed photo

Charles 'Chan' Channing Floyd preparing for a mission on the flight line at Bagram Air Base in Afghanistan.

Airman First Class Arlene Marie Perez-Rico on duty in Iraq in 2003.

Contributed by Sylvia Fuente

Contributed by Katherine Ontiveros Doyle

qi currency.

Contributed photo

Petty Officer Third Class Hector Baltazar Pena serves in the U.S. Navy. He enlisted in 2000. His tour has taken him aboard the aircraft carriers USS John C. Stennis and USS Carl Vinson.

Contributed photo

Cory Caswell (left) and Manuel J. Cavazos III both serve in the U.S. Navy. They enlisted in 1999. Their tours have taken them to Kuwait and Iraq.

Contributed

Jose H. Flores serves in the U.S. Marines. He enlisted in 2000 is on active duty.

Contributed by Sylvia Swift

rmy Sgts. Yolanda and Jonathan Swift with their baby, Samuel, in 2003. oth were with 101st Airborne and are now with the 1st Armored 1/1 Cav- alry. Sgt. Yolanda Swift is stationed at Hanau Base in Germany, and Sgt. Jonathan Swift is in Iraq with his unit from Budingen, Germany.

The Fuentes family

1968 – 1972

1966 ~ 1970

1965 – 1969

1966 – 1970

1972 – 1977   1973 – 1979   1957 – 1960   1975 – 1979   1976 – 1982

Contributed photo

The military veterans of the Fuentes family. From top left, counterclockwise: Ismael Fuentes, Ezequiel Fuentes, Rudolfo Fuentes, Alfonso Fuentes, David Fuentes, Enrique Fuentes, Marcos Fuentes, Richard Fuentes, and Israel Fuentes. Israel served in the Air Force. Richard and Israel served in Vietnam.

A tug boat assists the USS City of Corpus Christi, SSN-705, during its arrival at the Port of Corpus Christi in Dec. 1999. The nuclear-powered Los Angeles-class attack submarine was commissioned in 1983 and is homeported in Guam.

George Gongora/Caller-Times file

Joe Elizond
who served
the Marine
Corps from
1966 to 196
and his me

Contributed by Joe Elizondo

Portraits
of Heroes

A

Keith E. Abarca

Branch of service: Marines
Entered service: 1988
Discharge date: 1993
Places served: Japan, Saudi Arabia, Kuwait, Thailand, El Salvador
Highest rank: Staff sergeant
Decorations/ribbons: National Defense Medal, Marine Corps Service Medal, Combat Action Ribbon

Armando Abrego

Branch of service: Navy
Entered service: 1942

Kirk Andrew Abarca

Branch of service: Marine Reserves
Entered service: 1998
Discharge date: Currently serving
Places served: South America
Highest rank: Lance corporal

Jessie S. Abrego

Branch of service: Army

Robert Charles Abel

Branch of service: Navy
Entered service: 1974
Discharge date: 1978
Places served: United States
Highest rank: Petty officer second class
Decorations/ribbons: Good Conduct Medal

Pete Abrego

Branch of service: Army

Maynard Lynn Abrahams

Branch of service: Army Air Forces
Entered service: 1942
Discharge date: 1945
Places served: England
Highest rank: First lieutenant
Decorations/ribbons: DFC Air Medal with six Oak Leaf Clusters, five Battle Stars, Presidential Unit Citation

Arnold S. Acuna

Branch of service: Air Force
Entered service: 1951
Discharge date: 1955
Places served: Alaska
Highest rank: Staff sergeant

Edward S. Acuna

Branch of service: Air Force
Entered service: 1950
Discharge date: 1954
Places served: Korea
Highest rank: Sergeant

Daniel San Miguel Alaniz

A

Branch of service: Army
Entered service: 1941
Discharge date: 1945
Places served: United States, England and France
Highest rank: Private first class
Decorations/ribbons: Purple Heart

Rudy Oritio Adame

Branch of service: Army
Entered service: 1967
Discharge date: 1969
Places served: Japan and Louisiana
Highest Rank: E-5
Decorations/ribbons: National Defense Ribbon, Presidential Unit Good Conduct Ribbon

Francisco Alaniz Jr.

Branch of service: Marines
Entered service: 1966
Discharge date: 1968
Places served: Vietnam
Highest rank: Sergeant
Decorations/ribbons: National Defense Service Medal, Vietnam Service Medal with One Star, Vietnam Campaign Medal with Device, Purple Heart

Frank Z. Aguilar

Branch of service: Army
Entered service: 1943
Killed in action: 1944
Places served: France
Highest rank: Private first class
Decorations/ribbons: Two Purple Hearts

Ramiro A. Alejos

Branch of service: Army
Entered service: 1963
Discharge date: 1966
Places served: Germany
Highest rank: Sergeant
Decorations/ribbons: National Defense Medal, Rifle Sharpshooter Medal

Jose Aritia

Branch of service: Army
Entered service: 1965
Discharge date: 1967
Places served: Korea

James Robert Alty

Branch of service: Army
Entered service: 1950
Discharge date: 1952
Places served: Korea and Japan
Highest rank: Corporal
Decorations/ribbons: Good Conduct Medal, Korean Service Medal with two Bronze Stars, Combat Infantryman Badge

A

Andrew J. Anderson

Branch of service: Marines
Entered service: 1987
Discharged date: Currently serving
Places served: Texas

Roberto Gonzalez Anguiano

Branch of service: Army
Entered service: 1942
Places served: Normandy
Highest rank: Corporal
Decorations/ribbons: Two Bronze Stars, Purple Heart

David William Anderson Jr.

Branch of service: Marines
Entered service: 1984
Discharged date: Currently serving
Places served: Saudi Arabia and United States

Roberto Anguiano Jr.

Branch of service: Air Force
Entered service: 1966
Discharge date: 1986
Places served: Southeast Asia
Highest rank: Staff sergeant

Charles Lynn Andrews

Branch of service: Army
Entered service: 1968
Discharge date: 1970
Places served: Vietnam
Highest rank: Sergeant
Decorations/ribbons: Vietnam Campaign Medal, National Defense Service Medal, Vietnam Service Medal

Abel Aaron Arispe

Branch of service: Army
Entered service: 2000
Discharge date: Currently serving
Places served: Korea, Cuba and Iraq

Edward K. Andrews

Branch of service: Navy
Entered service: 1963
Discharge date: 1985
Places served: Vietnam, Iran, Grenada, Lebanon, Mexico and Virginia
Highest rank: Captain
Decorations/ribbons: Distinguished Flying Cross with one Bronze Star, Meritorious Service Medal, seven Air Medals

Roy H. Arispe

Branch of service: Army
Entered service: 1943
Discharge date: 1946
Places served: Normandy and the Rhineland
Highest rank: Technical sergeant fourth grade
Decorations/ribbons: WWII Victory Ribbon, Ribbon with three Bronze Service Stars, Rifle Marksman, Efficiency-Honor-Fidelity Medal

Antonio Arredondo Jr.

Branch of service: Army
Entered service: 1943
Discharge date: 1945
Places served: North Africa and Normandy
Highest rank: Private first class
Decorations/ribbons: Good Conduct Medal, three Overseas Service bars, EAME Campaign Medal with five Bronze Stars

Seberiano H. Arriola

Branch of service: Army
Entered service: 1941
Places served: Italy and Germany
Highest rank: Sergeant

Jesus N. Arredondo

Branch of service: Marines
Entered service: 1944
Discharge date: 1945
Places served: Japan
Highest rank: Private

Ben Avalos Jr.

Branch of service: Air Force
Entered service: 1948
Discharge date: 1952
Places served: Japan
Highest rank: Staff sergeant
Decorations/ribbons: Japan Occupation Medal, Good Conduct Medal

Manuel Arredondo

Branch of service: Army

Benjamin Rios Barajas

Branch of service: Army
Entered service: 1943
Discharge date: 1946
Highest rank: Sergeant
Places served: South Pacific

Jose C. Arellano

Branch of service: Army
Entered service: 1952
Discharge date: 1953
Places served: Korea

Benjamin Barajas Jr.

Branch of service: Army
Entered service: 1965
Discharge date: 1967
Highest rank: Sergeant
Places served: Panama Canal Zone

B

Arnulfo T. Barrera

Branch of service: Army
Entered service: 1940
Discharge date: 1944
Places served: France and England
Highest rank: Corporal
Decorations/ribbons:
Combat Infantryman Badge, European-African-Middle Eastern Theater Medal, Good Conduct Medal, Purple Heart

Eloy Barrera

Branch of service: Army
Entered service: 1940
Discharge date: 1944
Places served: Europe
Highest rank: Private first class

Emilio Barrera

Branch of service: Army
Entered service: 1940
Killed in action: 1941
Places served:
Philippines
Highest rank: Private first class

Evan Barrera

Branch of service: Army
Places served: European Theater and Korea
Highest rank: Private First Class
Decorations/ribbons:
Efficiency-Honor-Fidelity Medal, World War II Medal, EAME Campaign Medal, American Campaign Medal

George Trevino Barrera

Branch of service: Army Signal Corps
Entered service: 1942
Discharge date: 1946
Places served: India
Highest rank: Staff sergeant
Decorations/ribbons:
China-Burma-India Theater, Asiatic-Pacific Area, Good Conduct Medal, Victory Medal

Raul Trevino Barrera

Branch of service: Army
Entered service: 1942
Discharge date: 1945
Places served: England, France and Germany
Highest rank: Private first class
Decorations/ribbons:
EAME Campaign Medal with Two Bronze Stars, Good Conduct Medal, Four Overseas Service Bars

Rodolfo Trevino Barrera

Branch of service: Army Air Forces
Entered service: 1943
Discharge date: 1946
Places served:
New Jersey, Nebraska and Florida
Highest rank: Sergeant
Decorations/ribbons:
Victory Medal, Good Conduct Medal

William Trevino Barrera

Branch of service: Navy
Entered service: 1944
Discharge date: 1946
Places served: South Pacific
Decorations/ribbons: Four Battle Stars, American Area Campaign, Asiatic-Pacific Area, Philippines Liberation Medal, Good Conduct Medal and World War II Victory Medal

B

Leopoldo P. Barrientos

Branch of service: Army
Entered service: 1966
Discharge date: 1968
Places served: Germany, England, Georgia and Oklahoma
Highest rank: Private first class

Jimmy Ray Black

Branch of service: Army
Entered service: 1966
Discharge date: 1969
Places served: Germany
Highest rank: Specialist 5 — Sergeant

Candelario Bayarena Jr.

Branch of service: Army
Entered service: 1943
Discharge date: 1946
Places served: France
Highest rank: Private first class
Decorations/ribbons: World War II Victory Ribbon, Good Conduct Medal, American Theater Ribbon, EAME Theater Ribbon

Robert Marion Black

Branch of service: Navy
Entered service: 1942
Discharge date: 1945
Places served: Philippines
Highest rank: Aviation Machinist Mate Third Class

Eliazar Benavidez

Branch of Service: Navy

William Nicholas Bluntzer

Branch of service: Army Air Force
Entered service: 1943
Discharge date: 1946
Places served: India, Texas, Oklahoma, California, Arizona and Kansas
Highest rank: First lieutenant
Decorations/ribbons: Air Medal-DFC

Clifford (Bud) Allie Benson Jr.

Branch of service: Air Force
Entered service: 1950
Discharge date: 1955
Places served: Korea
Highest rank: First lieutenant
Decorations/ribbons: Air Medal, Korea Service Medal, National Defense Service Medal

Thomas Hilmon Bookout

Branch of service: Navy
Entered service: 1940
Discharge date: 1963
Places served: Iceland, England, North Africa and Puerto Rico
Highest rank: Captain

B

Jose A. Borciaga

Branch of service: Army
Entered service: 2000
Discharge date: Currently serving
Places served: Kuwait
Highest rank: Specialist

Bert A. Bottomstone

Branch of service: Army
Entered service: 1942
Discharge date: 1945
Places served: England and France
Highest Rank: Staff sergeant
Decorations/Ribbons: Good Conduct Medal, EAME Service Ribbon, Three Bronze Service Stars.

Catarino 'Nino' Botello

Branch of service: Army
Places served: World War II

Bill R. Brady

Branch of service: Navy
Entered service: 1942
Discharge date: 1946
Places served: South Pacific
Highest rank: Master chief petty officer

Rosalba Dolores Botello-Chambers

Branch of service: Army
Entered service: 1990
Discharge date: Currently serving
Places served: Hawaii, New York and Iraq
Highest rank: Sergeant First Class

Pat R. Brady

Branch of service: Army
Entered service: 1964
Discharge date: 1966
Places served: Korea and Vietnam
Highest rank: Private first class
Decorations/ribbons: Korea Medal, Vietnam Medal

Jose Albert Botello

Branch of service: Army
Entered service: 1992
Discharge date: 1999
Places served: Hawaii, New York and North Carolina
Highest rank: Personnel Administrator, E-4

Harold C. Brannies

Branch of service: Merchant Marines
Entered service: 1943
Discharge date: 1954
Places served: North Africa, Italy and France
Highest rank: Bosun

Robert (Brownie) Brownell

Branch of service: Navy instructor pilot
Places served: Texas
Highest rank: Instructor pilot

John Newton Brown IV

Branch of service: Marines
Entered service: 2002
Discharge date: Currently serving
Places served: United States, Iraq and Kuwait
Highest rank: Lance corporal

Richard A. Bryan

Branch of service: Air Force
Entered service: 1948
Discharge date: 1971
Places served: Philippines, Turkey, Germany, Korea, Vietnam
Highest rank: Master sergeant
Decorations/ribbons: Korea Service Medal, Good Conduct Medal, Vietnam Service Medal

Catarino Caballero

Branch of service: Army Air Forces
Entered service: 1942
Discharge date: 1945
Highest rank: Corporal

David Bridges

Branch of service: Navy (Seabees)
Entered service: 1951
Discharge date: 1955
Places served: Philippines
Highest rank: Petty officer second class
Decorations/ribbons: Philippines Service Ribbon, Korean Service Ribbon, Good Conduct Medal

Daniel Javier Caballero

Branch of service: Army
Entered service: 1995
Discharge date: Currently serving
Places served: Cuba, Iraq and Texas
Highest rank: Sergeant

Ernest R. Briones

Branch of service: Army
Places served: North Africa, China, Asiatic-Pacific Theater
Highest rank: Corporal

Reynaldo Caceres

Branch of service: Army
Entered service: 1954
Discharge date: 1970
Places served: Vietnam
Highest rank: Chief warrant officer 3

C

Robert Callejo

Branch of service: Marines
Entered service: 1967
Discharge date: 1968
Places served: Vietnam
Highest rank: E-4
Decorations/ribbons:
Purple Heart, Combat Action Ribbon, Presidential Unit Citation, Good Conduct Medal, National Defense Service Medal, Vietnam Service Medal

Robert Gordon Campbell

Branch of service: Air Force
Entered service: 1950
Discharge date: 1954
Places served: England, Florida and Mississippi
Highest Rank: Staff sergeant

Lazaro O. Camarillo III

Branch of service: Army
Entered service: 1968
Discharge date: 1970
Places served: Vietnam
Highest rank: Sergeant, E-5
Decorations/ribbons:
Bronze Star with "V" Device, two Army Commendation Medals with one Oak Leaf Cluster and one "V" Device, Marksman M-14, National Defense Service Medal

Sam Campbell

Branch of service: Army
Entered service: 1942
Discharge date: 1947
Places served: Europe and Italy
Highest rank: Captain

Harry Henderson Campbell

Branch of Service: Army

Jesse H. Campos Jr.

Branch of service: Army
Entered service: 1973
Discharge date: 1976
Places served: Texas
Highest rank:
Specialist 4
Decorations/ribbons:
National Defense Service Medal

James Alan Campbell

Branch of service: Army
Entered service: 1975
Discharge date: 1979
Places served: Germany
Highest rank: Private

Johnny H. Campos

Branch of service: Army
Entered service: 1974
Discharge date: 1976
Places served: Germany

C

Enrique Canales

Branch of service: Army
Air Forces
Entered service: 1942
Discharge date: 1945
Places served: Germany
Highest rank: Private

Noel Cantu

Branch of service: Army
Entered service: 1983
Discharge date: 1991
Places served: Germany,
Saudi Arabia, Iraq, Colorado
Highest rank: Staff sergeant
Decorations/ribbons: 82nd
Airborne Ranger, four
Army Achievement
Medals, two Good Con-
duct Medals, Combat
Infantry Badge, Senior
Parachutist Badge, Ranger
Tab, Airborne Wings

Juan Ramon Canales

Branch of service: Army
Discharge date: Current-
ly serving
Places served: Texas
Decorations/ribbons:
National Security
Award, National
Defense Medal, Expert
in M16, Expert in
Grenade, Expert in 50
Caliber, Expert in
Machine Gun

Rudy Cantu II

Branch of service: Army
Discharge date: 2001
Places served:
South Korea

Amelia G. Cantu

Branch of service: Army
Entered service: 1996
Discharge date: 1998
Places served: Germany
and the United States

Faustino Cardenas

Branch of service: Army
Entered service: 1942
Discharge date: 1945
Places served: Italy,
France, Germany and
Central Europe
Highest rank: TEC4 MD
Decorations/ribbons:
EAME Campaign
Medal with Six Bronze
Stars, Good Conduct
Medal, Bronze Star
Medal

Jennifer Marie Cantu

Branch of service: Navy
Entered service: 1995
Places served: United
States

Christy Hill Cardozo

Branch of service:
MASH unit — Medical
Entered service: 1990
Discharge date: 1993
Places served: Iraq

C

Eddie R. Carranza

Branch of service: Army
Entered service: 1963
Discharge date: 1966
Place of service: Germany
Highest rank: Specialist 4

Cristoval D. Castillo

Branch of service: Air Force
Entered service: 2001
Discharge date: Currently serving
Places served: Japan, Texas and Mississippi
Highest rank: First lieutenant

Veronica Carranza

Branch of service: Marines
Entered service: 2002
Discharge date: Currently serving
Places served: Kuwait
Highest rank: Lance corporal

Raul F. Castillo

Branch of service: Navy
Entered service: 1956
Discharge date: 1960
Places served: Japan, Okinawa, Hong Kong and the Philippines
Highest rank: Petty officer third class
Decorations/ribbons: Good Conduct Medal

Conrado G. Carrillo

Branch of service: Army
Entered service: 1942 or 1943
Discharge date: 1946 or 1947
Places served: World War II

Simeon G. Carrillo

Branch of service: Army
Entered service: 1942 or 1943
Discharge date: 1946 or 1947
Places served: Philippines
Highest rank: Corporal

Fernando G. Carrillo

Branch of service: Army Air Forces
Entered service: 1942 or 1943
Discharge date: 1946 or 1947
Places served: World War II

Charles Haiven Castro

Branch of service: Army
Entered service: 1944
Discharge date: 1946/1951
Places served: Germany
Highest rank: Private first class
Decorations/ribbons: Purple Heart, Silver Star

C

Frank G. Cavazos

Branch of service: Army
Entered service: 1943
Discharge date: 1945
Highest rank: Private
first class

Ramiro R. Chavez

Branch of service: Army
Entered service: 1967
Discharge date: 1969
Places served: Vietnam
Highest rank: Specialist 5
Decorations/ribbons: Bronze
Star, Purple Heart, Republic
of Vietnam Gallantry Cross
with Palm Unit Citation
Badge, Republic of Vietnam
Civil Actions Honor Medal

John O. Chapman Jr.

Branch of service: Army
Entered service: 1943
Discharge date:
1945 or 1946
Places served: England,
Germany and France
Highest rank: Sergeant

Roland Chavez

Branch of service:
Air Force
Entered service: 1988
Discharge date: 1991

George Chavez

Branch of service: Army
Entered service: 1973
Discharge date: 1993
Places served: South Korea,
Germany and Egypt
Highest rank: Sergeant first
class
Decorations/ribbons: Berlin
Occupational Medal, Army
Commendation Medal
with five Star Clusters,
Non-Commission Officers
Professional Ribbon,
Expert Infantry Badge

Ruben Chavez, Sr.

Branch of service: Army
Entered service: 1966
Discharge date: 1969
Places served: Vietnam
Highest rank: SPEC 4
Decorations/ribbons:
Vietnam Medal

John J. Chavez, Jr.

Branch of service: Air
Force
Entered service: 1965
Discharge date: 1969
Places served: Vietnam
and the Philippines
Highest rank: Senior
airman
Decorations/ribbons:
Good Conduct Medal,
Vietnam Ribbon,
Expert M-16

Ruben D. Chavez Jr.

Branch of service: Army
Entered service: 1987
Discharge date: 1991
Highest rank: Private
first class

C

Joseph A. Cisneros

Branch of service: Marines
Entered service: 1991
Discharge date: Currently serving
Places served: Iraq, Japan
Highest rank: Staff sergeant
Decorations/ribbons: Humanitarian Service Medal, Good Conduct Medal, Certificate of Commendation, numerous Letters of Appreciation.

George Albert Coleman

Branch of service: Army
Entered service: 1942
Discharge date: 1945

Marc Anthony Cisneros

Branch of service: Army
Entered service: 1961
Discharge date: 1996
Places served: Germany, Vietnam and Panama
Highest rank: Lieutenant general
Decorations/ribbons: Distinguished Service Medal, Legion of Merit, Bronze Star, Combat Infantry Badge

Augustin V. Collin

Branch of service: Navy
Entered service: 1967
Discharge date: 1969
Places served: Vietnam, Midway Island
Highest rank: Petty officer third class
Decorations/ribbons: Vietnam Service Medal, National Service Medal

Moises Cisneros

Branch of service: Army
Entered service: 1992
Discharge date: 2001
Places served: Germany, Arizona and Georgia
Highest rank: Sergeant
Decorations/ribbons: Basic Training Ribbon, Overseas Ribbon, Two Good Conduct Medals, Arial Avment Medal, Airborne Wings, Rigger Wings

Luis R. Corona

Branch of service: Army
Entered service: 1956
Discharge date: 1958
Places served: Germany
Highest rank: Sergeant
Decorations/ribbons: Good Conduct Medal

Ralph W. Cobb, Jr.

Branch of service: Navy Reserves
Entered service: 1942
Discharge date: 1962
Places served: NAS Dallas, USS Tarawa
Highest rank: Commander

Ramon Corona

Branch of service: Army
Entered service: 1967
Discharge date: 1969
Places served: Vietnam and Louisiana

Ramon L. Corona

Branch of service: Army
Entered service: 1957
Discharge date: 1959
Places served: Hawaii
Highest rank:
Specialist 5
Decorations/ribbons:
Good Conduct Medal

John Cruz

Branch of service: Army

Carl Washburn Crickenberger, Sr.

Branch of service: Army
Entered service: 1939
Discharge date: 1946
Places served: Europe
Highest rank: First
lieutenant
Decorations/ribbons:
Two Bronze Stars, two
Silver Stars with Oak
Leaf Clusters, Battle-
field Commission, eight
President's Citations,
numerous Unit Citations

Doyle Curtiss

Branch of service: Army
Places served: Korea
and Japan
Highest rank: Private

Alexander A. Crocker

Branch of service: Army
Entered service: 1984
Discharge date: Current-
ly serving
Places served: Sinai
Desert, Kosovo,
Yugoslavia,
United Nations
Peacekeeping Forces
Highest Rank: Staff
sergeant

Frederick George Culbertson Jr.

Branch of service: Army
Entered service: 1941
Discharge date: 1945
Places served: North
Africa, France and
Germany
Highest rank: Captain
Decorations/ribbons:
African and European
Theaters Campaign
Medals

Thomas M. Crocker

Branch of service: Army
Entered service: 1944
Killed in action: 1945
Places served: France and
Germany
Highest rank: Private
first class
Decorations/ribbons:
Purple Heart, three
Battle Stars

Rodolfo De La Cruz

Branch of service: Air
Force
Entered service: 1944
Discharge date: 1947
Places served: Japan
Highest rank: Private
first class
Decorations/ribbons:
Medal of Valor, Cross
for Valor

D

Joaquin A. De Leon

Branch of service: Army
Entered service: 2001
Discharge date:
 Currently serving
Places served: Iraq
Highest rank: Sergeant

Armando DeLeon

Branch of service: Army
Entered service: 1976
Discharge date: 1980
Highest rank: Second
 lieutenant
Decorations/ribbons:
 Reserve Officer Associ-
 ation Ribbon

Porfirio G. De Leon

Branch of service: Army
Places served: Germany
Highest rank: Private
 first class

Canderlario DeLeon, Jr.

Branch of service:
 Air Force
Entered service: 1965
Discharge date: 1968
Places served: Thailand
Highest rank: Staff
 sergeant
Decorations/ribbons:
 Presidential Unit Cita-
 tion Ribbon, Air Force
 Good Conduct Medal,
 Air Force Small Arms
 Expert

David Del Llano

Branch of service: Army
Entered service: 1955
Discharge date: 1956
Highest rank: Private
 first class

Canderlario DeLeon III

Branch of service: Marines
Entered service: 1995
Discharge date: 1999
Places served: U.S.
Highest rank: Corporal
Decorations/ribbons:
 Pistol Sharpshooter, Rifle
 Sharpshooter, two Navy
 and Marine Corps
 Achievement Medals,
 meritorious promotion
 twice, Letter of
 Appreciation

Henry Del Llano

Branch of service:
 Air Force
Entered service: 1941
Discharge date: 1963
Places served: Guadalcanal,
 South Pacific, Germany
 and North Africa
Highest Rank:
 Staff sergeant
Decorations/Ribbons:
 Bronze Star, American
 Campaign Freedom of
 Peace, European-African-
 Middle Eastern Campaign

Roberto DeLeon

Branch of service:
 Marines, Texas Army
 National Guard, Texas
 Air National Guard
Entered service: 1967
Discharge date: 2003
Places served: Vietnam
 and Puerto Rico
Highest rank: Captain
Decorations/ribbons:
 Purple Heart, Army
 Achievement Medal,
 RVN Service Medal
 with three Stars

D

Valentin DeLeon

Branch of service: Army
Entered service: 1967
Discharge date: 1971
Places served: Vietnam, Germany and Hawaii
Highest rank: Specialist fourth class
Decorations/ribbons: Combat Infantryman Badge, Bronze Star Medal, RVN Service Medal with three Stars, RVN Gallantry Cross Unit Citation Ribbon

Coy Lee Denton

Branch of service: Army Nurse Corps
Entered service: 1944
Discharge date: 1953
Places served: Philippines, Korea, Germany and Texas
Highest rank: Captain

Ismael (Milo) C. Diaz

Branch of service: Army
Entered service: 1966
Discharge date: 1969
Places served: Vietnam
Highest rank: Specialist fifth class

David Diaz

Branch of service: Army
Entered service: 1949
Discharge date: 1952
Places served: Korea
Highest rank: Sergeant first class
Decorations/ribbons: Five Battle Stars

Grant Leefe Deming

Branch of service: Navy
Entered service: 1941
Killed in action: 1951
Places served: Aleutian Islands
Highest rank: Petty officer first class
Decorations/ribbons: Good Conduct Medal

John A. Dittmar

Branch of service: Navy
Entered service: 1943
Discharge date: 1946
Places served: South Pacific, China, Iwo Jima, Okinawa and Japan
Highest rank: Pharmacist mate third class
Decorations/ribbons: Philippines Liberation Ribbon with Bronze Star

Gladys McCullough Deming

Branch of service: Naval Reserve — WAVES
Entered service: 1943
Discharge date: 1945
Places served: New York City, Oklahoma and Louisiana
Highest rank: Petty officer third class

John William Dominguez

Branch of service: Air Force
Entered service: 1962
Discharge date: 1971
Places served: England
Highest rank: Staff sergeant
Decorations/ribbons: National Defense Medal, Marksman Medal, Good Conduct Medal

D

Pete G. Dominguez

Branch of service: Army
Entered service: 1941
Discharge date: 1946
Places served: Philippines, Guadalcanal, South Pacific
Highest rank: Staff sergeant
Decorations/ribbons: Bronze Medal, American Campaign Freedom Peace Medal, European-African-Middle Eastern Campaign Medal

Robert Bruce Douglas

Branch of service: Navy
Entered service: 1944
Discharge date: 1946
Places served: Marshall Islands
Highest rank: Lieutenant junior grade

Roman 'Rocky' Dominguez

Branch of service: Army
Entered service: 1968
Discharge date: 1971
Places served: Vietnam
Highest rank: Specialist 5
Decorations/ribbons: National Defense Vietnam Service Medal, Vietnam Campaign Medal, Bronze Star, Army Commendation

Roger Scott Douglas

Branch of service: Navy Seabees
Entered service: 1966
Discharge date: 1968
Places served: Antarctica and Rhode Island
Highest rank: Seabee E-5

Joseph Bonner Dorsey

Branch of service: Army
Entered service: 1968
Discharge date: 1970
Places served: Vietnam
Highest rank: Captain
Decorations/ribbons: Bronze Star, Army Commendation Medal, Vietnam Service Medal, National Defense Medal

Katherine Ontiveros Doyle

Branch of service: Army
Entered service: 1994
Discharge date: Currently serving
Places served: Iraq

James R. Dougherty Jr.

Branch of service: Army
Places served: Germany
Highest rank: Lieutenant
Decorations/ribbons: Distinguished Service Cross

Wayne A. Dugger

Branch of service: Army
Entered service: 1946
Discharge date: 1949
Places served: Italy
Highest rank: Private first class

Gabrielle Renee Duran

Branch of service: Navy
Entered service: 2000
Discharge date:
Currently serving
Places served:
South Carolina
Highest rank: Petty officer third class

Edward L. Fasnacht

D-E-F

Branch of service Navy
Entered service:
1940 or 1941

Edgar H. Eggert, Jr.

Branch of Service:
Army Air Forces
Entered Service: 1943
Discharge Date: 1945
Places Served: Italy
Highest Rank: First lieutenant
Decorations/Ribbons:
Distinguished Flying Cross, Air Medal with three Oak Leaf Clusters, Pistoland Carbine Expert

James (Tino) A. Fasnacht

Branch of service: Navy
Entered service: 1940
Lost at sea: 1944
Places served: East China and Yellow Sea
Highest rank: Quarter master second class

Crispin T. Espinosa

Branch of service: Army
Entered service: 1942
Discharge date: 1945
Places served: Germany

Joseph A. Fasnacht

Branch of service: Army
Entered service: 1941
Killed in action: 1943
Places served:
Guadalcanal

Eric Lee Espinoza

Branch of service: Marines
Entered service: 1989
Discharge date: 1992
Places served: California, Philippines and North Carolina
Highest rank: Lance corporal
Decorations/ribbons: Good Conduct Medal, Presidential Unit Citation Medal, Rifle Sharpshooter, Pistol Sharpshooter

Samuel B. Fasnacht

Branch of service: Army
Entered service:
1941 or 1942
Places served: England, France, Germany

F

Armando H. Felix

Branch of service:
Marine Corps
Entered service: 1944
Killed in action: 1945
Places served: Iwo Jima
Highest rank: Private

Miguel Flores Jr.

Branch of service: Navy
Entered service: 1993
Discharge date: Currently serving
Places served: Kuwait, Iran, Persian Gulf and Australia
Highest rank: First class petty officer

Jose Felix

Branch of service: Army
Entered service: 1942
Discharge date: 1946
Places served: Belgium and Germany
Highest rank: Private first class
Decorations/ribbons: Bronze Star

Orlando S. Flores

Branch of service: Navy (Seabees)
Entered service: 1994
Discharge date: 2001
Places served: California and Florida
Highest rank: Petty officer second class
Decorations/ribbons: National Defense Medal, Expert M-16 Medal, two Navy "E" Ribbons

Ron Fledderman

Branch of service: Navy
Entered service: 1952
Discharged: 1976
Places served: Cuba, Puerto Rico, Sicily, Spain, Newfoundland, Texas, Florida, and New York
Highest rank: Chief personnelman
Decorations received: Navy Unit Commendation, Meritorious Unit Commendation, Navy Good Conduct Award

Ramiro Flores

Branch of service: Army, Air Force Reserves
Entered service: 1957, 1970
Discharge dates: 1963, 1996
Places served: Korea, Guam, Philippines, Thailand, Vietnam, Germany, Central America, Hawaii
Highest rank: Specialist 5
Decorations/ribbons: Army Good Conduct Medal, Small Arms Expert, Longevity Ribbons

Frank Flores Jr.

Branch of service: Army
Entered service: 1966
Discharge date: 1969
Places served: Vietnam
Highest rank: Staff sergeant
Decorations/ribbons: Purple Heart, Combat Infantry Badge, Bronze Star, Vietnam Service Medal, Good Conduct Medal

Ramiro Flores III

Branch of service: Air Force
Entered service: 1985
Discharge date: Currently serving
Places served: England, Saudi Arabia, Kuwait, Bosnia
Highest rank: Technical sergeant
Decorations/ribbons: Two Air Force Commendation Ribbons, two Air Force Achievement Medals, NCO Professional Ribbon

F

Raul Fuentes Flores

Branch of service: Marines
Entered service: 1965
Discharge date: 1966
Places served: Vietnam
Highest rank: Lance corporal
Decorations/ribbons: Purple Heart, Vietnam Service Medal, Republic of Vietnam Campaign Medal, Presidential Unit Commendation Ribbon, Combat Action Ribbon

Conrad Houston Floyd

Branch of service: Army
Entered service: 1958
Discharge date: 1961
Places served: Arkansas, Louisiana and France
Highest rank: Specialist 4
Decorations/ribbons: Good Conduct Medal, Expert Rifle

Maxine Edmondson Flournoy

Branch of service: WASP — Women Airforce Service Pilots
Entered service: 1943
Discharge date: 1944
Places served: Texas

George Franco

Branch of service: Navy
Entered service: 1993
Discharge date: 1999
Places served: Japan and the Philippines

Clayton W. Floyd

Branch of service: Army Air Forces
Entered service: 1940
Discharge Date: 1945
Places Served: Texas
Highest Rank: Master sergeant

Raul Franco

Branch of service: Army
Entered service: 1949
Discharge date: 1953
Places served: Korea
Highest rank: Corporal
Decorations/ribbons: Combat Infantryman Badge, Blue and Silver Emblem, Korean Service Medal with five Campaign Stars

Charles 'Chan' Channing Floyd

Branch of service: Air Force
Entered service: 1982
Places served: Iraq and Afghanistan
Highest rank: Lieutenant colonel
Decorations/ribbons: Bronze Star

Matthew Freitag

Branch of service: Army
Entered service: 1997
Discharge date: 2003
Places served: Georgia, South Carolina, Arizona, Italy, Germany, Kosovo, Kuwait and Iraq
Highest rank: Sergeant
Decorations/ribbons: Soldier of the Month

F-G

Felipe C. Fuentes

Branch of service: Army
Entered service: 1947
Places served: Korea
Highest rank: Staff sergeant
Decorations/ribbons:
United Nations Service Medal, Commendation Ribbon with Pendant, American Occupation Medal — Japan, Korean Service Medal, five Battle Stars

Fidel C. Fuentes

Branch of service: Army
Places served:
Philippines and Korea
Highest rank: Staff sergeant

Francisco C. Fuentes

Branch of service: Army
Entered service: 1952
Discharge date: 1973
Places served: Korea
Highest rank: First sergeant

Fred Fuentes

Branch of service: Army
Entered service: 1992
Discharge date: 1997
Places served: Panama, South Carolina, Indiana and Washington
Decorations/Ribbons:
Army Commendation Medal, Good Conduct Medal, Army Achievement Medal

Ruben Riojas Fuentes

Branch of service: Army
Entered service: 1974
Discharge date: 1994
Places served: Germany, Korea and Alaska
Highest rank: Sergeant first class
Decorations/ribbons:
MSM First Award, Army Commendation Medal, Good Conduct Medal, Army Achievement, Airborne Parachute Award

Erwin Otto Fuhrken

Branch of service: Army
Entered service: 1941
Discharge date: 1945
Places served: France, Germany and Central Europe
Highest rank: Sergeant
Decorations/ribbons:
Good Conduct Medal, Combat Infantryman Badge, two Bronze Stars with Oak Leaf Clusters, Purple Heart

Louis F. Gagniere

Branch of service: Navy
Entered service: 1942
Discharge date: 1950
Places served: South Pacific
Highest rank: Master chief
Decorations/ribbons:
Purple Heart

Noel H. Galindo

Branch of service: Army
Entered service: 1964
Discharge date: 1966
Places served: Germany

G

Ralph Galvan Jr.

Branch of service: Army
Entered service: 1943
Discharge date: 1946
Places served: Texas, Oklahoma, France, Germany and Austria
Highest rank: Technician 4th Grade
Decorations/ribbons: Good Conduct Medal, Efficiency, East Campaign Medal with two Battle Stars, World War II Medal

Sammie Galvan

Branch of service: Army
Entered service: 1943
Discharge date: 1946
Places served: Texas, France, Belgium and Germany.
Highest rank: Technician fourth grade
Decorations/ribbons: Efficiency, Fidelity & Honor American Campaign Medal, East Campaign Medal with one Battle Star, World War II Medal

Amando Garcia

Branch of service: Army
Branch of service: 1964
Discharge date: 1968
Places served: Germany and Vietnam
Highest rank: E6
Decorations/ribbons: Vietnam Service Medal

Antonio R. Garcia

Branch of service: Army
Entered service: 1965
Discharge date: 1967
Places served: Vietnam
Highest rank: Corporal

Armando M. Garcia

Branch of service: Army
Entered service: 1966
Discharge date: 1968
Places served: Germany
Highest rank: Sergeant

Benito Garcia

Branch of service: Army
Entered service: 1941
Killed in action

Catarino M. Garcia

Branch of service: Army
Decorations/ribbons: Purple Heart

Clemente G. Garcia

Branch of service: Air Force
Entered service: 1951
Discharge date: 1953
Places served: Illinois and Texas
Highest rank: Airman third class

G

Felix Longoria Garcia

Branch of service: Navy
Entered service: 1942
Discharge date; 1945
Places served: South Pacific Theater
Highest rank: Seaman first class
Decorations/ribbons: Good Conduct Medal, American Campaign Medal, Asiatic Pacific Campaign Medal

Ovidio Garcia Sr.

Branch of service: Army
Entered service: 1942
Discharge date: 1945
Places served: New Guinea, the Philippines and the South Pacific
Decorations/ribbons: Combat Infantry Badge, Asiatic Campaign Ribbons

Jacob Garcia

Branch of service: Air Force
Entered service: 1998
Discharge date: Currently serving

Ovidio Garcia Jr.

Branch of service: Army
Entered service: 1960
Discharge date: 1980
Places served: Vietnam, Germany and Japan
Highest rank: First sergeant
Decorations/ribbons: Combat Infantry Badge, Master Parachutist, Purple Heart, Bronze Star, Legion of Merit Vietnam Campaign Medals

Leonel Garcia

Branch of service: Army
Entered service: 1950
Discharge date: 1952
Places served: Germany
Decorations/ribbons: Army Occupational Medal

Ramiro D. Garcia

Branch of service: Army
Entered date: 1943
Discharge date: 1946
Places served: England, France, Germany and Holland
Highest rank: Corporal
Decorations/ribbons: Bronze Star, European Medal, Good Conduct Medal

Oscar H. Garcia

Branch of service: Army
Entered service: 1968
Discharge date: 1970
Place of service: Vietnam
Highest rank: Specialist 4
Decorations/ribbons: Expert Rifle M-14, Expert Rifle M-16, Vietnam Service Medal with three Bronze Stars, Army Commendation Medal, Combat Infantryman Badge, Air Medal

Robert E. Garcia

Branch of service: Army
Entered service: 1940
Discharge date: 1946
Places served: Philippines and New Guinea
Highest rank: Major

G

Robert Stillman Garcia

Branch of service: Navy
Entered service: 1941
Places served: Hawaii

Ruben Garcia

Branch of service: Army
Entered service: 1987
Discharge date: 1992
Places served: Kuwait, Germany and Iraq
Highest rank: Specialist fourth class
Decorations/ribbons: Army Commendation Medal, Army Good Conduct Medal, National Defense Medal, Saudi Arabian Liberation of Kuwait Medal, Kuwait Liberation Medal

Roberto Garcia

Branch of Service: Army

Ruben Garcia, Jr.

Branch of service: Navy

Rodolfo Stillman Garcia

Branch of service: Army
Entered service: 1941
Discharge date: 1945
Places served: Germany
Decorations/ribbons: Bronze Medal

Abel C. Garza

Branch of service: Army
Places served: Japan

Roel Garcia

Branch of service: Army

Efrain Garza Jr.

Branch of service: Air Force
Entered service: 2003
Discharge date: Currently serving
Highest rank: Airman

G

Frank J. Garza

Branch of service: Navy
Entered service: 1948
Discharge date: 1952
Places served: Japan
    and Korea
Highest rank: Seaman
Decorations/ribbons:
    Korean War Service
    Medal, Good Conduct
    Medal, Republic of Korea
    War Service Medal,
    Combat Action Ribbon,
    Republic of Korea
    Presidential Unit Citation

Richard Castillo Garza

Branch of service:
    Marines
Killed in action: 1950
Places served: Korea
Highest rank: Private
    first class

Joe J. Garza

Branch of service: Army
Service time: More than
    20 years
Killed in Iraq
Places served: Georgia,
    Germany and Iraq
Highest rank: First
    sergeant

John DeForest Gauss

Branch of service: Army
Entered service: 1941
Discharge date: 1945
Places served: South
    Pacific
Highest rank: Private
    first class

Margarito Garza

Branch of service: Marines
Entered service: 1966
Discharge date: 1967
Places served: Vietnam
Highest rank: Corporal
Decorations/ribbons: Military Merit Medal, Purple
    Heart, Rifle Sharpshooter, Rifle Expert, National
    Defense Medal, Gallantry
    Cross with Palm, Republic of Vietnam Service
    Medal

Edmond Hamilton Gentry

Branch of service: Navy
Entered service: 1940
Discharge date: 1966
Places served: South
    Pacific, Texas, Rhode
    Island, and Louisiana
Highest rank: Commander
Decorations/ribbons:
    Command at Sea
    Insignia, World War II
    Victory Medal, China and
    Korean Service Medals

Omar Garza

Branch of service:
    Marines
Entered service: 1993
Discharge date: 1995
Places served: Japan,
    Korea and California
Highest rank: Lance
    corporal
Decorations/ribbons: Sea
    Service Deployment
    Ribbon, Letter of
    Appreciation, Rifle
    Expert Third Award,
    Good Conduct Medal

Keith D. Gipson

Branch of service: Army
Entered service: 1986
Discharge date: Currently
    serving
Places served: Germany,
    Bosnia, Kuwait, Iraq, Michigan, New Jersey and Texas
Highest rank: Staff sergeant
Decorations/ribbons: NCO
    Professional Development
    Second Award, four Army
    Commendation Medals,
    seven Army Achievement
    Medals

Kevin R. Gipson

Branch of service: Air Force, Air Force Reserves
Entered service: 1986 and 1992
Discharged date: 1992 and 1996
Places served: Turkey, Saudi Arabia, Korea, Italy, Germany, Georgia, Texas, Oklahoma, New Jersey and California
Highest rank: Staff sergeant

Feliciano Gomez Jr.

Branch of service: Army
Entered service: 1997
Places served: Italy and Germany
Highest rank: Sergeant

G

James R. Glover

Branch of service: Army
Entered service: 1940
Discharge date: 1944
Places served: Germany
Decorations/ribbons: Good Conduct Medal, Presidential Unit Emblem, American Defense Service Medal, American Campaign Medal, European-African-Middle Eastern Campaign Medal, Bronze Star, World War II Victory Medal

Amado M. Gonzales

Branch of service: Army
Entered service: 1968
Discharge date: 1971
Places served: Vietnam
Highest rank: Sergeant
Decorations/ribbons: Bronzed Star, Purple Heart, Combat Infantry Badge

John Gollihar, Jr.

Branch of service: Navy
Entered service: 1941
Discharge date: 1946
Places served: South Pacific, Texas and Midway
Highest rank: Chief petty officer

Geronimo J. Gonzales

Branch of service: Marines
Entered service: 1967
Discharge date: 1969
Places served: Vietnam
Highest rank: Lance corporal
Decorations/ribbons: National Defense Service Medal, Purple Heart

Armando Gomez

Branch of service: Army
Entered service: 1955

Jose E. Gonzales

Branch of service: Army
Entered service: 1942
Discharge date: 1943
Places served: Germany
Highest rank: Private
Decorations/ribbons: Good Conduct Medal

G

Luis Gonzales

Branch of service: Army
Entered service: 1977
Discharge date: 1979
Places served: Germany

Duane Gonzalez

Branch of service: Air Force
Entered service: 1990
Discharge date: Currently serving
Places served: Philippines, Germany and Russia

Reynaldo Gonzales

Branch of service: Army
Entered service: 1956
Discharge date: 1959
Places served: Georgia, Missouri and California

Fructoso A. Gonzalez

Branch of service: Marines
Entered service: 1969
Discharge date: 1973
Highest rank: Staff sergeant
Decorations/ribbons: Purple Heart

Valentin B. Gonzales

Branch of service: Army
Entered service: 1950
Discharge date: 1953
Places served: Germany
Highest rank: Staff sergeant
Decorations/ribbons: Expert Infantry Badge, Good Conduct Medal, Victory Medal

Gilbert Gonzalez III

Branch of service: Marines
Entered service: 1985
Discharge date: 1994
Places served: Desert Shield/Storm, North Carolina, California, Arizona and Texas
Highest rank: Sergeant
Decorations/ribbons: National Defense Ribbon, Meritorious Promotion to Lance Corporal, Rifle Expert Ninth Award

Crespiniano V. Gonzalez

Branch of service: Army
Entered service: 1934
Discharge date: 1940
Highest rank: Sergeant

Jesus Gonzalez

Branch of service: Army
Entered service: 1942
Discharge date: 1946
Places served: Asiatic Pacific, Europe, and the Solomon Islands
Highest rank: Sergeant first class
Decorations/ribbons: Asiatic-Pacific Campaign Medal with One Bronze Star, American Campaign Medal, Good Conduct Medal, World War II Medal

G

Jesus A. Gonzalez

Branch of service:
Marines
Entered service: 1960
Discharge date: 1967
Highest rank:
Staff sergeant

Mariano O. Gonzalez

Branch of service:
Marines
Entered service: 1969
Discharge date: 1971
Highest rank: Sergeant

John J. Gonzalez

Branch of service: Army
Places served:
Philippines, North
Africa and Japan

Noe J. Gonzalez

Branch of service: Army
Entered service: 1990
Discharge date: Current-
ly serving
Places served: United
States
Highest rank: Sergeant

Jose Gonzalez

Branch of service: Army
Entered service: 1974
Discharge date: 1980
Places served: Korea,
North Carolina, South
Carolina and Louisiana
Decorations/ribbons:
Expert Rifle Medal

Oliveros Gonzalez

Branch of service: Army
Entered service: 1946
Discharge date: 1947
Places served: Germany
Highest rank: Sergeant

Juan Gonzalez

Branch of service: Army
Places served: South
Pacific
Highest rank: Private
first class

Xavier F. Gonzalez

Branch of service:
Air Force
Entered service: 1957
Discharge date: 1961
Places served: North
Africa
Decorations/ribbons:
Good Conduct Medal

G

Alexander G. Grande

Branch of service: Marines
Entered service: 1942
Discharge date: 1967
Places served: Korea, Vietnam, Guadalcanal and Alaska
Highest rank: Staff sergeant
Decorations/ribbons: Presidential Unit Citation Ribbon with one Star, WWII Victory Medal, three Bronze Stars, two Silver Stars

Jack Jerome Grant

Branch of service: Marines
Entered date: 1942
Killed In action: 1944
Places served: South Pacific
Highest rank: Private first class

Donald Anthony Grant

Branch of service: Navy
Entered service: 1945
Discharge date: 1946
Places served: California
Highest Rank: Seaman first class
Decorations/ribbons: American Area Campaign, WWII Victory

Lester D. Grant

Branch of service: Marines
Entered service: 1944
Discharge date: 1946
Place of service: Pearl Harbor
Highest rank: Corporal
Decorations/ribbons: Asiatic Pacific Area, Good Conduct Medal, Victory Medal

Forest Jacob Grant

Branch of service: Army
Entered service: 1942
Discharge date: 1946
Places served: South Pacific and the Philippines
Highest rank: Staff sergeant
Decorations/ribbons: Asiatic Pacific Area, Philippines Liberation, Good Conduct Medal, WWII Victory Medal

Merald Bernard Grant

Branch of service: Army
Entered service: 1942
Discharge date: 1946
Places served: North Africa and Italy
Highest rank: Sergeant
Decorations/ribbons: Good Conduct Medal, American Campaign, European African Middle Eastern Medal, WWII Victory Medal

Gerald C. Grant

Branch of service: Army
Entered service: 1943
Discharge date: 1946
Places served: North Africa, Italy and California
Highest rank: Sergeant
Decorations/ribbons: American Campaign, Middle Eastern Area Medal, Good Conduct Medal, WWII Victory Medal

William B. Grantham

Branch of service: Navy
Entered service: 1942
Discharge date: 1975
Places served: USS Bennington, Iwo Jima, Okinawa and Texas
Highest rank: Chief
Decorations/ribbons: Good Conduct, Navy Reserve, Asiatic Pacific, American Defense Service, European-African Campaign

Bernard B. Grossman

Branch of service: Army
Entered service: 1942
Discharge date: 1946
Places served: Pacific Theater
Highest rank: Captain

Juan C. Guerrero

Branch of Service: Army
Entered Service: 1942
Discharge Date: 1945
Places Served: Italy
Highest Rank: Private first class
Decorations/Ribbons: EAME Campaign Medal with four Bronze Stars, Good Conduct Medal, Victory Ribbon, one Service Stripe, five Overseas Service Bars

G

Emilio G. Guerrero

Branch of service: Army
Entered service: 1948
Discharge date: 1952
Highest rank: Corporal

Ruperto G. Guerrero

Branch of service: Army
Entered service: 1943
Discharge date: 1946
Places served: Asiatic Pacific Theater of Operations

Lucio Guajardo Jr.

Branch of service: Army
Entered service: 1971
Discharge date: 1991
Places served: Panama, South America, Vietnam and United States
Highest Rank: Staff sergeant

Victor Guerrero

Branch of service: Army
Entered service: 1962
Discharge date: 1966
Places served: Vietnam
Highest rank: Fourth Class Specialist Engineer

Lucio Guajardo III

Branch of service: Army
Entered service: 1995
Discharge date: Currently serving
Places served: Egypt and Hawaii
Highest rank: Staff sergeant, E-6

Tillman Morgan Gunn

Branch of service: Marines
Entered service: 1942
Discharge date: 1945
Highest rank: First Class Sharpshooter

G-H

Genaro G. Gutierrez

Branch of service: Army
Entered service: 1947
Discharge date: 1949
Places served: California
Highest rank: Corporal

Warren K. Guy

Branch of service: Navy
Entered service: 1940
Discharge date: 1945
Places served: Hawaii
Highest rank: Naval
  cadet

Gregorio G. Gutierrez

Branch of service:
  Marines
Entered service: 1951
Discharge date: 1962
Places served: Hawaii,
  Japan and Okinawa
Highest rank: Sergeant
Decorations/ribbons:
  United Nations Medal,
  Good Conduct Medal

Jesse James Hale, Sr.

Branch of service: Army
Entered service: 1942
Discharge date: 1946
Places served: Philippines
Highest rank: Sergeant
Decorations/rank: American
  Theater Campaign Medal,
  Good Conduct Medal,
  Asiatic Pacific Campaign
  Medal with one Bronze Star,
  Victory Ribbon, Philippine
  Liberation Ribbon

Lauro G. Gutierrez

Branch of service:
  Marines
Entered service: 1958
Discharge date: 1962
Places served: Japan and
  Okinawa
Highest rank: Corporal

Marvin Monroe Hall

Branch of service: Army
Entered service: 1943
Discharge date: 1945
Places served:
  Philippines
Highest rank: Private
  first class
Decorations/ribbons:
  Purple Heart

Manuel Gutierrez

Branch of service: Army
  Air Forces
Entered service: 1942
Discharge date: 1946
Highest rank: Staff
  sergeant
Decorations/ribbons:
  Asiatic-Pacific Campaign
  Medal, American Theater
  Campaign Medal, Good
  Conduct Medal, World
  War II Victory Medal

David R. Headley

Branch of service: Army
Entered service: 1967
Discharge date: 1987
Places served: Vietnam
  and Germany
Highest rank: Chief
  warrant officer
Decorations/ribbons:
  Two Purple Hearts,
  Meritorious Service
  Medal, Bronze Star,
  Air Medal

H

Manuel M. Hernandez

Branch of service: Air Force
Entered service: 1951
Discharge date: 1991
Highest rank: Master sergeant

Juan Ayon Hinojosa

Branch of service: Army
Entered service: 1954
Discharge date: 1956
Places served: Germany
Highest rank: Private first class

Abel V. Herrera

Branch of service: Marines
Entered service: 1989
Discharged: 1993
Places served: United States and Kuwait
Highest rank: Corporal
Decorations received: Combat Action, Kuwait Liberation, Southwest Asia, National Defense, Sea Service Deployment, Good Conduct

Ladislao Hinojosa Jr.

Branch of service: Army
Entered service: 1967
Discharge date: 1973
Places served: Vietnam, Louisiana, Oklahoma, and Maryland
Highest rank: Sergeant
Decorations/ribbons: Vietnam Campaign Medal, O/S Bars, Marksman Badge Rifle M-14, Expert Badge Rifle M-16, Bronze Star

Baltazar Herrera, Jr.

Branch of service: Navy
Entered service: 1968
Discharge date: 1974
Places served: Vietnam
Highest rank: Petty officer second class
Decorations/ribbons: National Defense Medal, Navy Unit Citation, Combat Action Medal, Gallantry Medal with Oak Leaf Device, Good Conduct Medal

James Patrick Hill

Branch of service: Navy
Entered service: 1944
Discharge date: 1945
Places served: South Pacific Theater
Highest rank: Quartermaster

Albert E. Hesseltine Sr.

Branch of service: Army
Places served: New Guinea
Highest rank: Staff sergeant

Charles A. Hoffman

Branch of service: Navy
Entered service: 1976
Discharge date: 1988
Places served: Philippines and the South Pacific
Highest rank: Weapons technician first class
Decorations/ribbons: Navy Commendations, Navy Achievement Medal, Good Conduct Medal

H-I-J

Harry Hoffman

Branch of service: Navy
Entered service: 1942
Discharge date: 1946
Places served:
South Pacific
Highest rank:
Navy medic
Decorations/ribbons:
Victory Medal, Good
Conduct Medal, Asiatic
Pacific Medal, American
Theater Medal, Expert
Marksman

Marion H. (Red) Isaacks

Branch of service: Navy
Entered service: 1951
Discharge date: 1978
Places served:
Mediterranean, Western
Pacific and Vietnam
Highest rank: Captain
Decorations/ribbons:
Silver Star, two Bronze
Stars, Meritorious Ser-
vice Medal

Walter B. Hopkins

Branch of service: Army
Entered service: 1985
Discharge date: 1990
Places served: Germany
and the United States
Highest rank: Sergeant
Decorations/ribbons:
Master Rifle, Soldier of
the Month

Gary Lee Jackson

Branch of service: Air
Force
Entered service: 1989
Places served: Mississip-
pi
Decorations/ribbons:
Letter of Commenda-
tion

Lloyd (Pete) H. Hughes

Branch of service: Army
Air Forces
Entered service: 1942
Killed in action: Aug. 1,
1943
Places served: Africa
Highest rank: First
lieutenant
Decorations/ribbons:
Congressional Medal of
Honor, Purple Heart

Nelson Wade Jackson Sr.

Branch of service: Army
Entered service: 1954
Discharge date: 1958
Places served: New Jersey
and Pennsylvania
Highest rank: Specialist 3
Decorations/ribbons:
Good Conduct Medal,
National Defense
Service Medal

Robert Henry Hunt

Branch of service: Army
Air Forces
Entered service: 1942
Discharge date: 1945
Places served: North Africa
and England
Highest rank: Flight engineer
Decorations/ribbons: Air
Medal with two Oak Leaf
Clusters, Purple Heart,
European Theater Medal
with nine Bronze Stars,
Good Conduct Medal

Nelson Wade Jackson Jr.

Branch of service: Air
Force
Entered service: 1989
Discharge date: Currently
serving
Places served: Korea, Texas
and Washington, D.C.
Highest rank: Staff sergeant
Decorations/ribbons:
Professional Military
Ribbon, Longevity
Ribbon, Overseas Ribbon,
Good Conduct Medal

T. M. Jarvis Jr.

Branch of service: Army
Entered service: 1944
Discharge date: 1946
Places served: France
and Germany
Highest rank: Private
first class
Decorations/ribbons:
Two Purple Hearts

Alfonso R. Jimenez

Branch of service: Army
Entered service: 1942
Discharge date: 1945
Places served: Italy and
Tunisia
Highest rank: Private
first class
Decorations/ribbons:
EAME Campaign
Medal with three
Bronze Stars, Good
Conduct Medal

J

Leobardo M. Jaurigui

Branch of service:
Air Force
Entered service: 1967
Discharge date: 1969
Places served: Germany
Highest rank:
Staff sergeant

Helen Robinson Jiral

Branch of service:
Auxiliary Women's
Army Corps

Jerry P. Jenkins

Branch of service: Army
Entered service: 1943
Discharge date: 1945
Places served: California
Highest rank: First
lieutenant
Decorations/ribbons:
American Theater
Ribbon, Victory Medal,
Army Aviation Wings

James Ballard Johnson

Branch of Service: Army
Air Forces
Entered Service: 1942
Discharge Date: 1946
Places Served: Japan
Highest Rank: Sergeant

Joe Jessel

Branch of service: Navy

Bernard Jones

Branch of service:
Army Reserves
Entered service: 2001
Discharge date:
Currently serving
Places served: Kuwait

H-I-J

Clarice B. Jones

Branch of service:
Air Force
Entered service: 1944
Discharge date: 1946
Places served: Iowa
Highest rank: Private
first class
Decorations/ribbons:
Good Conduct Medal,
Permanent Party Medal

Matthew Stephen Koszubinski

Branch of service: Navy
Entered service: 1996
Discharge date:
Currently serving
Places served:
Washington, D.C.,
Texas and Illinois
Highest rank: Seaman
Decorations/ribbons:
ESWOS, Junior Sailor
of the Year 2002

Rolf R. Jorgenson

Branch of service:
Air Force
Entered service: 1954
Discharge date: 1977
Places served: Texas
Highest rank: Captain
Decorations/ribbons:
Good Conduct Medal

Vernon Krause

Branch of service: Army
Entered service: 1944
Discharge date: 1946
Highest rank:
Staff sergeant
Decorations/ribbons:
EAME Campaign
Medal with two Bronze
Stars, Good Conduct
Bronze Star Medal,
Distinguished Unit
WWII Victory Medal

Kenneth Martinez Juarez

Branch of service: Army
Entered service: 1994
Discharge date: 2003
Places served: Germany,
Haiti, Egypt, Korea and
Colorado
Decorations/ribbons:
Army Commendation
Medals, Joint Service
Achievement Medal,
Army Achievement
Medals, Marksmanship
Qualification Badge
with Rifle Bar

John Tidemand Kubsch

Branch of service: Navy
Entered service: 1998
Discharge date:
Currently serving
Places served:
Mediterranean Sea
Highest rank:
Petty officer second
class

David Lee Kelley

Branch of service: Army
Entered service: 1967
Discharge date: 1970
Places served: Vietnam
Highest rank:
Specialist 5
Decorations/ribbons:
Expert Rifle M-14

Matthew LaChapella

Branch of service: Navy
Entered service: 1993
Discharge date:
Currently serving
Places served: Florida
and Virginia
Highest rank: Lieutenant
junior grade

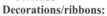

Jesse N. Laing

Branch of service: Army
Entered service: 1940
Discharge date: 1945
Places served: NorthAfrica, Italy, France, Austria, Belgium and Germany
Highest rank: Corporal
Decorations/ribbons: Purple Heart, Victory Medal WWII, American Defense Medal, Presidential Unit Citation, Good Conduct Medal, seven Battle Stars, two Arrowheads

Leonard D. Lance

J

Branch of service: Navy
Entered service: 1944
Discharge date: 1946
Places served: Washington, D.C.
Highest rank: Third class metalsmith

Raul Ruben Lamas

Branch of service: Army
Entered service: 1949
Killed in action: 1968
Places served: Korea, Germany, France and Vietnam
Highest rank: Sergeant first class
Decorations/ribbons: Purple Heart

William (Billy) Lance

Branch of service: Navy
Entered service: 1941
Discharge date: 1946
Places served: Hawaii
Highest rank: Petty officer first class

Victor Jose Lamas

Branch of service: Navy
Entered service: 1942
Discharge date: 1945
Places served: South Pacific and the Philippines
Highest rank: Pharmacist mate third class

Louis Lara Jr.

Branch of service: Navy
Entered service: 1961
Discharge date: 1964
Places served: California

J. R. Lance

Branch of service: Navy
Entered service: 1943
Discharge date: 1946
Places served: South Pacific, Philippines and Japan
Highest rank: Seaman first class
Decorations/ribbons: American Area, Asiatic Pacific Area with one Star, Philippines Liberation with one Star, Victory Ribbon, Good Conduct Ribbons

Harold Edward Larsen

Branch of service: Army Air Forces
Entered service: 1942
Discharge date: 1946
Places served: Germany and Central Europe
Highest rank: Captain
Decorations/ribbons: Bronze Star, Air Medal and one Oak Leaf Cluster, American Defense Service Ribbon, World War II Victory Medal

L

Harold Edward Larsen Jr.

Branch of service: Navy
Entered service: 1971
Discharge date: 1977
Places served: Vietnam and the Philippines
Highest Rank: Petty officer second class
Decorations/Ribbons: Vietnam Service Medal, Meritorious Unit Commendation, Navy Unit Commendation, and First Good Conduct Award

Larry N. Ligon

Branch of service: Air Force
Entered service: 1943
Discharge date: 1945
Places served: Guadalcanal, Admiralty Islands, New Guinea and the Philippines
Highest rank: Technical sergeant
Decorations/ribbons: Air Medals with three Oak Leaf Clusters, Purple Heart with one Oak Leaf Cluster, Asiatic Pacific Service Medal, Philippine Liberation Medal

Rev. Joseph R. Lawless

Branch of service: Army
Entered service: 1944
Discharge date: 1946
Places served: England, France, Germany and Austria
Highest rank: Captain
Decorations/ribbons: European Theater, Central Europe, Presidential Unit Citation, Bronze Star, Combat Infantry Badge

Mike Lira

Branch of service: Army
Entered service: 1998
Places served: Iraq and Kuwait

Juan Manuel Ledesma

Branch of service: Army
Entered service: 1963
Discharge date: 1965
Places served: Vietnam
Highest rank: Specialist 4
Decorations/ribbons: Vietnam Service Medal, Vietnam Campaign Medal, Combat Infantry Badge

Francis Marrion Logan

Branch of service: Army (Special Forces)
Entered service: 1963
Killed in action: Nov. 4, 1969
Places served: Vietnam
Highest rank: Staff sergeant
Decorations/ribbons: Silver Star (posthumously)

Frank G. Lemos

Branch of Service: Army Air Forces
Places Served: Guam and the Pacific Theater
Highest Rank: Corporal

Allen James Longoria

Branch of service: Army
Entered service: 2002
Discharge date: Currently serving
Places served: Kuwait and Iraq
Highest rank: Private first class

L

Esequiel Flores Longoria

Branch of service: Army
Entered service: 1979
Discharge date: 1986
Places served: Germany and Korea

Matt Longoria

Branch of service:
Air Force
Entered service: 1972
Discharge date: 1978
Places served:
United States
Highest rank: Sergeant
Decorations/ribbons:
National Defense Medal, Air Force Outstanding Unit Ribbon

Felix Longoria

Branch of service: Army
Entered service: 1944
Kill in action: 1945
Places served: Philippines
Highest rank: Private first class
Decorations/ribbons:
Purple Heart, Bronze Star

Matthew Joseph Longoria

Branch of service: Army
Entered service: 1994
Places served:
United States
Highest rank: Private first class

Mateo Longoria Jr.

Branch of service: Army
Entered service: 1955
Discharge date: 1956
Highest rank: Private

Mauro Longoria

Branch of service: Army
Entered service: 1944
Discharge date: 1946
Places served:
Philippines, South Pacific and New Guinea
Highest rank: Private first class
Decorations/ribbons:
Purple Heart, Good Conduct Medal, Expert Marksman, Philippine Liberation Medal

Matias Longoria Sr.

Branch of service: Army
Entered service: 1943
Discharge date: 1945
Places served: Philippines and New Guinea
Decorations/ribbons:
Pacific Campaign, National Defense Medal, Philippine Liberation Medal

Mauro Longoria Jr.

Branch of service:
Air Force
Entered service: 1967
Discharge date: 1971
Places served: Vietnam
Highest rank: Sergeant
Decorations/ribbons:
Expert Marksmen, Vietnam, Member of Honor Guard

L-M

Moses R. Longoria

Branch of service:
  Army Air Forces
Entered service: 1942
Discharge date: 1944
Places served: Germany
Highest rank: Sergeant
Decorations/ribbons:
  Good Conduct Medal

Melvin Lopez

Branch of service:
  Air Force
Entered service: 1963
Discharge date: 1969
Highest rank: Airman
  first class

Noe R. Longoria

Branch of service:
  Marines
Entered service: 1943
Discharge date: 1945
Places served: Japan
Highest rank: Sergeant
Decorations/ribbons:
  Good Conduct Medal

Octavio R. Luna

Branch of service: Army
Entered service: 1943
Discharge date: 1946
Places served: Italy and
  France
Highest rank: Medical
  corpsman

Victor Flores Longoria

Branch of service: Army
Entered service: 1975
Discharge date: 1981
Places served:
  United States

Jerry W. Lunceford

Branch of service: Navy
Entered service: 1972
Discharge date: 1980
Places served: Philip-
  pines, Japan, Vietnam,
  Pakistan
Highest rank: Petty
  officer first class
Decorations/ribbons:
  Vietnam Ribbon

Jose Antonio Lopez

Branch of service: Army
Entered date: 1998
Discharge date: 2002
Places served: Texas and
  Kentucky
Highest Rank: Corporal
Decorations/Ribbons:
  Presidential Unit Cita-
  tion, Army Achievement
  Award, High Pistol, Dri-
  vers Badge, Good Con-
  duct Medal, Three-year
  Service Stripe

Robert B. McKinley

Branch of service: Navy
Entered service: 1941
Discharge date: 1962
Places served: Texas and
  Kansas
Highest rank: Chief,
  Aviation Mechanist
  Mate

Casten John Mackerer

Branch of service: Army
Entered service: 1994
Discharge date: Currently serving
Places served: Korea, Turkey and Iraq
Highest rank: Specialist 4

Isidro Marquez

M

Branch of service: Air Force
Entered service: 1970
Discharge date: 1974
Places served: Vietnam
Highest rank: Sergeant
Decorations/ribbons: Air Medal, Air Force Commendation Medal, Presidential Unit Citation Ribbon, RVN Service Medal, Air Force Small Arms Expert, RVN Gallantry Cross Unit Citation Ribbon, RVN Campaign Medal with Date Bar

Kelly Glenn Maiden

Branch of service: Marines
Entered service: 1992
Discharge date: Currently serving
Places served: Panama, California, Hawaii
Highest rank: Sergeant
Decorations/ribbons: Navy Achievement, Selected Marine Corps Reserve Medal, National Defense Medal

Fidencio Martinez Jr.

Branch of service: Army
Entered service: 1998
Highest rank: Corporal

Gregory Nelson Maisel

Branch of service: Marines
Entered service: 1970
Discharge date: 1999
Places served: Beirut, Grenada, Panama, Iraq
Highest rank: Colonel
Decorations/ribbons: Meritorious Service Medal, Strike Flight Air Medal Three Awards, Navy Commendation Medal, Navy Achievement, Combat Action Ribbon

James Martinez

Branch of service: Navy
Entered service: 2001
Discharge date: Currently serving
Places served: Kuwait
Highest rank: Petty officer third class

Roberto Maldonado

Branch of service: Marines
Entered service: 1941
Discharge date: 1945
Places served: Guadalcanal
Highest rank: Private first class

Jason Martinez

Branch of service: Navy
Entered service: 2000
Discharge date: 2003
Highest rank: Petty officer third class

M

Jesse M. Martinez

Branch of service: Marines
Entered service: 1983
Discharge date: Currently serving
Places served: Japan, the Philippines, Kuwait, Iraq
Highest rank: Gunnery sergeant
Decorations/ribbons: Navy Achievement Medal

Quelfido Martinez

Branch of service: Army
Entered service: 1942
Discharge date: 1945
Places served: France and Germany
Highest rank: PVC, military police
Decorations/ribbons: Lapel Button

Jesus M. Martinez

Branch of service: Army
Entered service: 1945 and 1950
Discharge dates: 1948 and 1951
Places served: Germany and Korea
Decorations/ribbons: Victory Medal, Army of Occupation Medal, Good Conduct Medal, Purple Heart, Korean Service Medal with three Bronze Stars

Reyes Martinez II

Branch of service: Army
Entered service: 1970
Discharge date: 1976
Places served: Germany
Decorations/ribbons: Sharpshooter Medal

Mauricio R. Martinez

Branch of service: Marines
Entered service: 1958
Discharge date: 1968
Places served: Vietnam, Philippines and Japan
Highest rank: Staff sergeant
Decorations/ribbons: Navy/Marine Corps Commendation with Combat "V"

Adan O. Mendez

Branch of service: Army
Entered service: 1951
Discharge date: 1953
Places served: Germany
Highest rank: Private first class
Decorations/ribbons: German Occupation Ribbon, Marksman

Noe Martinez

Branch of service: Navy
Entered service: 1955
Discharge date: 1957
Places served: California
Highest rank: Seaman apprentice

Manuel Mendez

Branch of service: Army
Entered service: 1942 and 1946
Discharge dates: 1945 and 1949
Places served: Belgium and Germany
Highest rank: Sergeant
Decorations/ribbons: American Theater Campaign Medal, EAME Campaign Medal with three Bronze Stars, Good Conduct Medal, Victory Ribbon

Martin Mendez Jr.

Branch of service: Army
Entered service: 2000
Discharge date:
Currently serving
Places served: Iraq and New York
Highest rank: Private first class

Jesse Joe Mireles

Branch of service: Army
Entered service: 1966
Discharge date: 1967
Places served: Vietnam
Highest rank: Sergeant

M

Raul Mendez

Branch of service: Marines
Entered service: 1945
Discharge date: 1986
Places served: Japan, North China, Guam and Korea
Highest rank: Master sergeant
Decorations/ribbons: Good Conduct Medal, Combat Ribbon, Korea with two Bronze Stars, USMCR Medal, National Defense Medal

Xavier Paul Mireles

Branch of service: Air Force
Entered service: 1987
Discharge date: 1991
Places served: Saudi Arabia
Highest rank: Senior airman

Samuel Mendez

Branch of service: Air Force
Entered service: 1975
Discharge date: 1979
Places served: United States
Highest rank: Senior airman
Decorations/ribbons: Small Arms Marksman

Darrell Wayne Mokry

Branch of service: Navy
Entered service: 1988
Discharge date:
Currently serving
Places served: California, Nevada and Florida
Highest rank: Petty officer first class
Decorations/ribbons: Good Conduct Medal, Sea Service Ribbon

Gilbert Mireles

Branch of service: Marines
Entered service: 1953
Discharge date: 1983
Places served: Korea and Vietnam
Highest rank: Sergeant major
Decorations/ribbons: Navy Commendation Medal with Combat V, Vietnam Service Medal with four Battle Stars, Combat Action Ribbon and seven campaign ribbons

William (Bill) Dwight Mooney

Branch of service: Navy
Entered service: 1955
Places served: Japan and Vietnam
Highest rank: Chief petty officer
Decorations/ribbons: Navy Commendation Medal

M

Jose Antonio Montalvo

Branch of service: Army
Entered service: 1942
Places served: Holland, Belgium, France and Germany
Highest rank: Military police

Lisa Marie Mora

Branch of service: Marines
Entered service: 1992
Discharge date: 1995
Places served: School of Infantry, Marine Barracks 8th & I
Highest rank: Corporal
Decorations/ribbons: Good Conduct Medal, National Defense Medal, Meritorious Unit Commendation

Xavier Montalvo

Branch of service: Army Active Reserves
Places served: Panama
Highest rank: Lieutenant colonel

Sylvester Richard Mora

Branch of service: Marines
Entered service: 1988
Discharge date: 1999
Places served: Kuwait, North Carolina and Iraq
Highest Rank: Staff sergeant
Decorations/Ribbons: Navy Achievement Medal, Good Conduct Medal, Humanitarian Service Medal, Kuwait Liberation Medal,

David Montoya

Branch of service: Navy
Entered service: 1972
Discharge date: 1994
Places served: Iceland, Spain, Azores, Bermuda, California, Western Pacific and Persian Gulf
Highest rank: Lieutenant commander
Decorations/ribbons: Navy Commendation Medal, Operation Desert Storm Medal, National Defense Medal

Samuel Morales

Branch of service: Army
Places served: Germany and South Pacific
Highest rank: Corporal

Luis A. Montoya

Branch of Service: Navy
Entered Service: 1945
Discharge Date: 1946
Highest Rank: Seaman second class

Ernest Moreno

Branch of service: Air Force, Air Force Reserves
Entered service: 1969 and 1990
Discharge date: Currently serving
Places served: Desert Storm, Mississippi, Arizona and Florida
Highest rank: Master sergeant

Joe Moya Sr.

Discharge date: 1960
Places served: Korea
Highest rank: Specialist 5

Oscar P. Navejar

Branch of service: Army
Entered service: 1969
Discharge date: 1971
Places served: Texas
Highest rank: First
lieutenant
Decorations/ribbons:
Good Conduct Ribbon

M-N

Mike Muncy

Branch of service: Army
Entered service: 1970
Discharge date: 1974
Places served: Vietnam
Highest rank: Sergeant
Decorations/ribbons:
Army Commendation
Medal, Vietnam Cam-
paign Medal, Vietnam
Service Medal, Bronze
Star, Purple Heart,
Army Air Medal

Charles A. Nichols

Branch of service:
Marines
Entered service: 1943
Discharge date: 1946
Places served: South
Pacific
Highest rank: Corporal

Daniel Munguia

Branch of service: Army
Entered service: 1990
Discharge date: 1991
Places served:
Saudi Arabia
Highest rank: Sergeant
first class

Mitchell Frederic Nielsen

Branch of service: Army
Entered service: 1951
Discharge date: 1953
Places served: Germany
Highest rank: Corporal

Jose M. Naranjo

Branch of service: Army
Entered service: 1942
Discharge date: 1946
Places served: Texas,
Arkansas and Hawaii
Highest Rank: Private first
class
Decorations/Ribbons:
American Theater
Campaign Medal, Asiatic
Pacific Campaign Medal,
Good Conduct Medal, one
Service Stripe, three
Overseas Service Bars

Esteban Nieto

Branch of service:
Marines
Discharge date: 1963
Places served:
Philippines and Japan
Highest rank: Private
first class
Decorations/ribbons:
Marksman

N-O

Clifton Brooks Noel

Branch of service: Navy
Entered service: 1941
Discharge date: 1960
Places served: USS Casablanca, USS Coral Sea, USS Legte, USS Franklin D. Roosevelt
Highest rank: ADC, Aviation machinist mate chief
Decorations/ribbons: Philippines Liberation Medal, American Service Medal, Good Conduct Medal

Adolfo T. Olivarez

Branch of service: Army
Entered service: 1952
Discharge date: 1954
Highest rank: Private first class

Otto D. O'Brien

Branch of service: Army Air Forces
Entered service: 1943
Discharge date: 1945
Places served: France, Italy and North Africa
Highest rank: Sergeant

Martin Olivarez

Branch of service: Air Force
Entered service: 1984
Discharge date: 1985
Places served: Texas

Wilfred A.G. O'Brien

Branch of service: Royal Air Force V.R.
Highest rank: Wing commander
Decorations/ribbons: Order of the British Empire

Juan J. Ontiveros

Branch of service: Army
Entered service: 1943
Discharge date: 1945
Places served: France, Belgium and Holland
Highest rank: Private first class
Decorations/ribbons: Purple Heart

Loyd Raymond Oakes

Branch of service: Army Air Forces
Entered service: 1945
Places served: Korea
Highest rank: Major

Frank Ortiz

Branch of service: Army
Entered service: 1970
Discharge date: 1972
Places served: Vietnam
Decorations/ribbons: Vietnam Service Medal with two Bronze Stars, Vietnam Campaign Medal with 1960 Device, two C/S Bars, Good Conduct Medal (First Award), Purple Heart, Combat Infantryman Badge (First Award)

O

Horacio Ortiz

Branch of service: Army
Entered service: 1942
Discharge date: 1945
Places served: Normandy, Omaha Beach, Belgium (Battle of the Bulge)
Highest rank: Sergeant
Decorations/ribbons: Purple Heart, Combat Infantry Badge, European Campaign Medal, Good Conduct Medal

Joseph Frank Padilla, Sr.

Branch of service: Navy
Entered service: 1968
Discharge date: 1972
Places served: Vietnam and California
Decorations/ribbons: Southwest Asia, Sea Service, National Defense Medal

Jose Roberto Ortiz

Branch of service: Air Force
Entered service: 1961
Discharge date: 1964
Places served: Germany, New York, New Jersey, and Texas
Highest rank: Airman second class

Joseph Frank Padilla III

Branch of service: Navy
Entered service: 1988
Discharge date: 1993
Places served: California and Virginia
Highest rank: Petty officer third class
Decorations/ribbons: Good Conduct Medal, Sea Service Medal, South East Asia with Bronze Star, Unit Mention with Oak Cluster

Philip Coronado Ortiz

Branch of service: Army
Entered service: 1944
Discharge date: 1945
Places served: Philippines and Okinawa
Highest Rank: Private first class
Decorations/Ribbons: Asiatic Pacific Campaign Medal with two Bronze Stars, Philippine Liberation Ribbon with one Bronze Star

Pablo Padilla

Branch of service: Army
Entered service: 1967
Discharge date: 1969
Places served: Vietnam
Highest rank: Sergeant

Richard Eric Ortiz

Branch of service: Navy and Navy Reserves
Entered service: 1995
Discharge date: 1998
Places served: Bosnia, Virginia and USS Portland
Decorations/ribbons: Sea Service, National Defense, Good Conduct, Navy Battle E, Humanitarian Service Medal, Good Conduct Reserves

Mia Joyce Palacios

Branch of service: Army
Entered service: 2001
Places served: Iraq
Highest rank: Private first class

O-P

John M. Panek

Branch of service: Navy
Entered service: 1972
Discharge date: 2002
Decorations/ribbons:
Navy Commendation Medal, Navy and Marine Corps Achievement Medal, Navy Unit Citation, Good Conduct Medal, National Defense Service Medal, Kosovo Campaign Medal, Joint Meritorious Unit Award

Manuel Pena

Branch of service: Army
Entered service: 1969
Discharge date: 1971
Places served: Vietnam
Highest rank: Specialist 4
Decorations/ribbons:
National Defense Service Medal, Vietnam Service Medal with two Bronze Stars, Republic of Vietnam Campaign Medal, Expert Rifle Medal

Eugene E. Pasahow

Branch of service: Navy
Entered service: 1955
Discharge date: 1977
Places served: Japan, Vietnam, Maryland, Virginia and California
Decorations/ribbons:
Purple Heart, Combat Action, Good Conduct, Vietnam Campaign

Rudy 'Tejano' Pena

Branch of service: Navy
Entered service: 1964
Discharge date: 1995
Places served: Mediterranean Sea, Middle East, Southeast Asia, Vietnam, Australia, Guam, Persian Gulf, the Philippines and the Dominican Republic
Highest rank: Petty officer first class

Richard R. Paz

Branch of service: Army and U.S. Coast Guard
Entered service: 1969
Discharge date: 1991
Places served: Vietnam, Korea and Germany
Highest rank: Sergeant first class
Decorations/ribbons:
Bronze Star, Army Commendation Medal with two Oak Leaf Clusters, Army Achievement Medal with two Oak Leaf Clusters

Alejo I. Perez

Branch of service: Army
Entered service: 1949
Discharge date: 1953
Places served: Japan
Highest rank: Staff sergeant

Jesus R. Pena

Branch of service: Army
Entered service: 1942
Discharge date: 1945
Places served: Tunisia and Italy
Highest rank: Private first class, heavy machine gunner
Decorations/ribbons:
Bronze Star, Purple Heart, EAME Campaign Medal with five Bronze Stars

Eduardo P. Perez

Branch of service: Army
Entered service: 1940
Discharge date: 1946
Places served: Aleutian Islands (Alaska)
Highest rank: Army technical sergeant

P

Esequiel S. Perez

Branch of service: Army
Entered service: 1944
Discharge date: 1946
Places served: Japan and
Philippines
Highest rank: Private
first class

Pete M. Perez

Branch of service:
National Health
Service Corps
Entered service: 1994
Discharge date:
Currently serving
Places served: Virginia
and Texas
Highest rank: Commander

Hector R. Perez

Branch of service: Army
Entered service: 1980
Killed in action: July 2003
Places served: Germany,
Kosovo, Korea and Iraq
Highest rank: Staff ser-
geant
Decorations/ribbons: Three
ARCOM's, three AAM's,
four Good Conduct
Medals, NATO Medal,
NATO Service Medal
(Yugoslavia), Kosovo
Campaign Medal, EIB,
Bronze Star, Purple Heart

Robert C. Perez

Branch of service: Army
Entered service: 1945
and 1950
Discharge date: 1949
and 1953
Places served: Germany
and Korea
Highest rank: First
sergeant
Decorations/ribbons:
Purple Heart, Silver
Star, Korean Medal

Pedro C. Perez

Branch of service: Army
Entered service: 1945
Discharge date: 1946
Places served: Germany
Highest rank: Private
first class
Decorations/ribbons:
European Theater
of Operations

Romulo C. Perez

Branch of service: Army
Entered service: 1944
Discharge date: 1948
Places served: Italy
and the Philippines
Highest rank: Private

Pedro Ramon Perez

Branch of service: Army
Entered service: 1944
Discharge date: 1946
Places served: Germany
Highest rank: Private first
class
Decorations/ribbons:
EAME Campaign Medal
with one Bronze Star,
Good Conduct Medal,
Purple Heart, World War
II Victory Medal

Arlene Marie Perez-Rico

Branch of service:
Air Force
Entered service: 2000
Discharge date: Currently
serving
Places served: Iraq
Decorations/ribbons:
12th Security Forces
Airman of the Quarter,
Support Group Airman
of the Quarter, 12th
Flying Training Wing
Airman of the Quarter

P

Harlan Perrenot

Branch of service: Navy
Places served: California

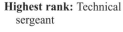

Frank Pizana

Branch of service: Air Force
Entered service: 1995
Places served: Iraq
Highest rank: Corporal

Robert Lloyd Perrenot

Branch of service: Navy
Entered service: 1942
Discharge date: 1945
Places served: South Pacific, Texas and California
Decorations/ribbons: Distinguished Flying Cross, four Air Medals

Manuel R. Pizana

Branch of service: Air Force
Entered service: 1949
Highest rank: Technical sergeant

Roberto Pina

Branch of service: Marines
Entered service: 1952
Discharge date: 1979
Places served: Korea, Japan, Philippines and Okinawa
Highest rank: Master sergeant
Decorations/ribbons: Three U.S. Navy Achievement Medals for Debriefing of U.S. POWs 1975, Special Operations for U.S. Border Patrol, 1978

Loren Wesley Plummer Jr.

Branch of service: Marines
Entered service: 1943
Discharge date: 1945
Places served: South Pacific
Highest rank: Sergeant
Decorations/ribbons: Silver Star, Presidential Citation, Purple Heart, Asiatic Pacific Medal

Andrew Pitts

Branch of service: Navy
Entered service: 1940
Places served: Kansas and Texas
Highest rank: Air traffic controller

Robert V. Poe Jr.

Branch of service: Army
Entered service: 1966
Places served: Germany
Highest rank: Specialist 4

Joe A. Pons

Branch of service: Army
Places served: South Pacific and Guam
Highest rank: Private first class

Jesus Fernando Quintanilla

P

Branch of service: Marines
Entered service: 1967
Discharge date: 1973
Places served: Vietnam
Highest rank: Lance corporal
Decorations/ribbons: Good Conduct Medal, Vietnam Service Ribbon, Vietnam Combat Ribbon with Two Clusters, Presidential Unit Citation

Johnny G.

Branch of service: Army
Entered service: 1941
Discharge date: 1945
Places served: Texas and France
Highest rank: Sergeant
Decorations/ribbons: Bronze Star, two Purple Hearts

Michael Radela

Branch of service: Army
Entered service: 2001
Places served: South Korea
Highest rank: Specialist 4

James Norman Price Jr.

Branch of service: Air Force
Entered service: 1941
Discharge date: 1961
Places served: Guadalcanal, north and south Pacific
Highest rank: Lieutenant colonel
Decorations/ribbons: Distinguished Flying Cross Air Medal

Abraham I. Ramirez

Branch of service: Navy
Entered service: 1989
Discharge date: 1996
Places served: Hawaii, Somalia, Central America
Highest rank: Lieutenant commander
Decorations/ribbons: National Defense Ribbon with Star, Navy Achievement Medal, Navy Commendation with two Gold Stars

Jesus Hernandez Pulido

Branch of service: Army
Entered service: 1943
Discharge date: 1945
Places served: Europe and Germany
Highest rank: Private
Decorations/ribbons: World War II Occupation of Germany, European-African-Middle Eastern Campaign, Bronze Star, Sharpshooter

Andres M. Ramirez

Branch of service: Navy
Entered service: 1942
Discharge date: 1946
Places served: Guadalcanal and Alaska
Highest rank: Second class builder
Decorations/ribbons: American Victory

P-R

George Ramirez

Branch of service: Army
Entered service: 1975
Discharge date: 1978
Places served: Germany, Louisiana and Texas
Highest rank: Specialist 4
Decorations/ribbons: Overseas Ribbon, Service Ribbon

Michael S. Ramirez Jr.

Branch of service: Navy
Entered service: 1963
Discharge date: 1967
Places served: Europe, Norway and the Dominican Republic

James V. Ramirez

Branch of service: Marines
Entered service: 2001
Discharge date: 2002
Places served: California
Highest rank: Private first class

Miguel L. Ramirez

Branch of service: Army
Entered service: 1941
Discharge date: 1945
Places served: England, France, Belgium, Holland and Germany
Highest rank: Sergeant
Decorations/ribbons: World War II Victory Medal, Marksman Medal, Honorable Service Lapel, American Defense Medal

Jose A. Ramirez

Branch of service: Army
Entered service: 1967
Discharge date: 1968
Places served: Vietnam
Highest rank: Specialist 4
Decorations/ribbons: Purple Heart

Ramiro P. Ramirez

Branch of service: Army
Entered service: 1964
Discharge date: 1968
Places served: Vietnam
Highest rank: Private first class radioman
Decorations/ribbons: Vietnam Medal of Honor

Joseph Paul Ramirez

Branch of service: Marines
Entered service: 2001
Discharge date: Currently serving
Places served: Iraq and North Carolina
Highest rank: Lance corporal

Samuel Ramirez

Branch of service: Army
Entered service: 1978
Discharge date: 1992
Places served: Germany, Turkey, Panama, and El Salvador
Highest rank: Major
Decorations/ribbons: Meritorious Service Medal, Army Commendation Medal, Expert Infantry Badge, Senior Parachutist Badge, Wings

R

Ysrael B. Ramirez

Branch of service: Army
Entered service: 1969
Discharge date: 1970
Places served: Vietnam
Highest rank: Sergeant
Decorations/ribbons:
Purple Heart, Life Membership of Military Order of the Purple Heart, Disabled American Veterans

Catarino E. Reyes

Branch of service:
Marines
Entered date: 1967
Discharge date: 1969
Places served: Vietnam and California
Highest rank: Corporal
Decorations/ribbons:
Combat Action Ribbon, Good Conduct Medal, National Defense Service Medal, Expert Rifle Badge

Julio Roberto Ramos

Branch of service: Army, Army National Guard
Entered service: 1994, 1997
Discharge date: 1997, currently serving
Places served: Oklahoma, Colorado and Texas
Highest rank: Sergeant
Decorations/ribbons: Army Achievement Medal, Good Conduct Medal, Army Reserve Components Achievement Medal

Juan Reyes

Branch of service: Army
Entered service: 1951
Discharge date: 1953
Places served: Korea
Highest rank: Corporal
Decorations/ribbons:
Korean Service Medal with three Bronze Service Stars, United Nations Service Medal

Jose Enrique Ramos

Branch of service: Army
Entered service: 1971
Discharge date: 1995
Places served: Germany, Honduras, Vietnam, Texas and Georgia
Highest rank: Sergeant
Decorations/ribbons:
National Defense Ribbon, Humanitarian Ribbon, Army Achievement Medal

John Paul Reyes

Branch of service: Navy
Entered service: 1994
Discharge date: 1999
Places served:
Mediterranean and Europe

Adan F. Rangel

Branch of service: Army
Entered service: 1943
Discharge sate: 1946
Places served: Philippines, South Pacific, New Guinea
Highest rank: Private first class
Decorations/Ribbons:
Good Conduct Medal, Asiatic Pacific Campaign Ribbon with two Bronze Stars, Philippine Liberation Ribbon with one Bronze Star

Roberto S. Reyes

Branch of service: Army
Entered service: 1954
Discharge date: 1976
Places served: Korea, Germany, Thailand and Vietnam
Highest rank: Sergeant first class

R

George Hugo Ritter

Branch of Service: Navy
Entered Service: 1941
Discharge Date: 1945
Places Served: Virginia

James D. Robbins

Branch of service: Army
Entered service: 1957
Discharge date: 1995
Places served: Germany, Korea, El Salvador, Vietnam, Saudi Arabia and Kuwait
Highest rank: Chief warrant officer 4

Joseph Arthur Ritter

Branch of service: Army
Entered service: 1943
Discharge date: 1945
Places served: France and Germany
Highest rank: Private first class
Decorations/ribbons: Bronze Star, Purple Heart with Oak Leaf Cluster

Dr. James M. Robinson Jr.

Branch of service: Army Air Forces
Highest rank: Lieutenant

David R. Rivas

Branch of service: Marines
Entered service: 1974
Discharge date: 1994
Places served: Japan, North Carolina and Hawaii
Highest rank: Gunnery sergeant
Decorations/ribbons: Naval Achievement Medal, National Defense Medal with Bronze Star, Good Conduct Medal with four Stars, Navy Commendation Medal

Emilio Rodela Jr.

Branch of service: Army
Entered service: 1965
Discharge date: 1967
Places served: Vietnam
Highest rank: Corporal
Decorations/ribbons: Purple Heart

Lowell Thomas (Tom) Roach

Branch of service: Army
Entered date: 1951
Discharge date: 1953
Places served: Korea
Highest rank: Corporal

Amado Rodriguez

Branch of service: Army
Entered service: 1943
Discharge date: 1946
Places served: New Guinea and the Philippines
Highest rank: Technician fifth grade
Decorations/ribbons: American Ribbon, Asiatic-Pacific Theater Ribbon, Philippine Liberation Medal, Good Conduct Medal

B. Frank Rodriguez

Branch of service: Army
Discharge date: 1955
Places served: Korea
Highest rank: Sergeant
Decorations/ribbons:
Korean Service Medal with two Bronze Stars, National Defense Service Medal, United Nations Service Medal, Command Infantry Badge

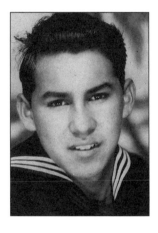

Edward Rodriguez

Branch of service: Navy

John V. Rodriguez

Branch of service: Army
Entered service: 1942
Discharge date: 1945
Places served: Philippines, New Guinea and northern Solomons
Highest rank: Private first class
Decorations/ribbons:
Asiatic-Pacific Campaign Medal with three Bronze Stars, Philippines Liberation Ribbon with one Bronze Star

Juan Rodriguez

Branch of service: Air Force
Entered service: 1969
Discharge date: 1976
Places served: Philippines and Korea
Highest rank: Sergeant

Luis Rodriguez

R

Branch of service: Army
Entered service: 1952
Discharge date: 1981
Places served: Korea, Germany and Vietnam
Highest rank: E-8
Decorations/ribbons:
Bronze Star with V Device and one Oak Leaf Cluster, American Defense one Oak Leaf, Korean Service Medal with two Bronze Stars, four Bronze Stars

Mark Anthony Rodriguez

Branch of service: Army
Entered service: 1985
Discharge date: 1993
Places served: Korea, Iraq, Kuwait and United States
Highest rank: Sergeant
Decorations/ribbons:
Three Army Achievement Medals, Good Conduct Medal, Expert M-16 Rifle Medal

Maximo Rodriguez

Branch of service: Marines
Places served: Vietnam

Orlando Javier Rodriguez

Branch of service: Army
Entered service: 2001
Discharge date: Currently serving
Places served: South Korea and North Carolina

R

Roberto R. Rodriguez

Branch of service: Marines
Entered service: 1969
Discharge date: 1972
Places served: Greece, Spain and Portugal
Highest rank: Lance corporal

Julius Marks Rosenberg

Branch of service: Army
Entered service: 1943
Discharge date: 1945
Places served: New Guinea, Philippines and Japan
Highest Rank: Private first class
Decorations/ribbons: Four D-Day Landing Ribbons

Salvador Rodriguez

Branch of service: Army
Highest rank: Private first class

Jose Ruelas

Branch of service: Army
Entered service: 1943
Discharge date: 1946
Places served: Philippines and the South Pacific
Highest rank: Technician fifth grade

Ruben E. Rosales

Branch of service: Marines
Entered service: 1959

Mateo Ruelas

Branch of service: Army
Entered service: 1969
Killed in action: 1970
Places served: Vietnam
Highest rank: Specialist 4

Larry Rose

Branch of service: Army
Entered service: 1966
Discharge date: 1969
Places served: Georgia, New Jersey, Germany and Vietnam

Ray Runnels

Branch of service: Army
Entered service: 1974
Discharge date: 1977
Places served: Texas
Highest rank: Specialist 4
Decorations/ribbons: Expert Shooter Badge, National Defense Medal

Rodney O'Neal Runnels

Branch of service: Navy
Entered service: 1988
Discharge date:
Currently serving
Places served:
Persian Gulf and Iraq
Highest rank: Petty
officer first class

Jose Alfredo Salazar

R-S

Branch of service: Army
Entered service: 2000
Discharge date:
Currently serving
Places served: Kosovo
and Afghanistan
Highest rank: Sergeant
Decorations/ribbons:
Kosovo Campaign
Medal, Army Achieve-
ment Medal, Army
Commendation Medal,
Good Conduct Medal

Alvaro D. Saenz

Branch of service: Army
Air Forces
Places served: Nevada
Highest rank: Sergeant

Joseph Salazar

Branch of service:
Air Force
Entered service: 1999
Discharge date:
Currently serving
Places served: Germany
and Japan

Raul P. Saenz

Branch of service: Army
Places served:
Philippines and Guam
Highest rank: Private

Luis Chapa Salazar

Branch of service: Army
Entered service: 1942
Discharge date: 1945
Places served:
Philippines and
South Pacific
Highest rank: Corporal

Albert Anthony Salazar

Branch of service: Marines
Entered service: 1988
Discharge date: 1993
Places served: Philippines,
Desert Storm/Shield
and California
Highest rank: Corporal
Decorations/ribbons:
Navy Achievement
Medal, Combat Action
Ribbon, Meritorious Unit
Citation, Rifle & Pistol
Expert Ribbon

Roger P. Salazar

Branch of service: Army
Discharge date: 1945
Places served:
Philippines
Highest rank: Private
first class

S

Vicente C. Salazar

Branch of service: Army
Entered service: 1941
Discharge date: 1945
Highest rank: Private first class
Decorations/ribbons: Purple Heart

Oswaldo Lopez Salinas

Branch of service: Air Force
Entered service: 1941
Discharge date: 1971
Places served: Italy, North Africa, Korea and Vietnam
Highest rank: Staff sergeant
Decorations/ribbons: Bronze Star, Rifling, Parachuting

Carlos Salinas

Branch of service: Marines
Entered service: 2003
Discharge date: Currently serving

Rogelio Salinas

Branch of service: Army
Entered service: 1966
Discharge date: 1972
Places served: Vietnam and Germany
Highest Rank: Sergeant
Decorations/ribbons: Purple Heart, Bronze Star, Army Campaign Medal, Vietnam Campaign Medal, Airborne Badge, Combat Infantry Badge

Jose Salinas

Branch of service: Army
Entered service: 1951
Discharge date: 1952
Places served: Korea

Ruben Salinas

Branch of service: Marines
Entered service: 1947
Discharge date: 1954
Places served: Korea
Highest rank: Staff sergeant
Decorations/ribbons: Presidential Unit Citation, Korean Medal, Good Conduct Medal, Pacific Theater, Purple Heart, Expert Marksmanship

Omar V. Salinas

Branch of service: Army
Entered service: 1955
Discharge date: 1957
Places served: Korea and Japan
Highest rank: Specialist 3

Andy Sanchez

Branch of service: Army
Entered service: 1995
Discharge date: Currently serving
Places Served: South Korea, Kuwait, Iraq
Highest rank: Captain
Decorations/ribbons: Army Commendation Medal with Oak Leaf Cluster, Army Achievement Medal, Army Parachutist's Badge, Army Air Assault Badge

S

Orlando Julio Sanchez

Branch of service: Army Air Forces
Entered service: 1942
Discharge date: 1945
Places served: Europe
Highest rank: Staff sergeant
Decorations/ribbons: European Theater Operations Ribbon, six campaign stars, Air Medal with three Oak Leaves, three Unit Citations

Willie Lee Schlinke

Branch of service: Army
Entered service: 1940
Discharge date: 1945
Places served: North Africa, Italy and France
Highest rank: Sergeant
Decorations/ribbons: EAME Campaign Medal with five Bronze Stars, Bronze Indian Arrowhead, Good Conduct Medal, American Defense Service Medal

Ronald Vernon Satre

Branch of service: Navy — Merchant Marines
Entered service: 1942
Discharge date: 1944
Places served: Pacific
Highest rank: Radarman third class

Charles Dennis Scott

Branch of service: Army
Entered service: 1942
Discharge date: 1945
Places served: Europe, France, England and Czechoslovakia
Decorations/ribbons: European Theater Campaign, Normandy — Central Europe Campaign

Margaret Jean Schrot

Branch of service: Army Nurse Corps
Entered service: 1942
Discharge date: 1945
Places served: European Theater
Highest rank: Lieutenant

Bernard Jerome Seal

Branch of service: Army
Entered service: 1946
Discharge date: 1949
Places served: Germany
Highest rank: Lieutenant

Charles Edward Schlinke

Branch of service: Navy
Entered service: 1970
Discharge date: 1990
Places served: Italy, Iceland, United Kingdom, United States
Highest rank: Radioman first class
Decorations/ribbons: Good Conduct Medal, Sea Service, National Defense with Star

John Albert Seeber

Branch of service: Army
Entered service: 1938
Discharge date: 1958
Places served: Germany
Highest rank: Major

S

Mauro Ramos Serrano

Branch of service: Army
Entered service: 1940
Discharge date: 1944
Places served: Germany
  (POW) and Texas
Highest rank: Patrol
  leader, staff sergeant
Decorations/ribbons:
  Prisoner of war

Jerry W. Simmons

Branch of service:
  Air Force
Entered service: 1953
Discharge date: 1957
Places served: Mississippi,
  Massachusetts and
  Tennessee
Highest rank: Airman first
  class

Anastacio Silva

Branch of service: Navy
Entered service: 1944
Discharge date: 1945
Places served:
  United States
Highest rank: Seaman
Decorations/ribbons:
  Good Conduct Medal

Charles L. Skrobarczyk

Branch of service:
  Air Force
Places served:
  United States
Highest rank: Corporal

Eric Daniel Silva

Branch of service:
  Marines
Entered service: 1999
Discharge date:
  Currently serving
Places served: Iraq
Highest rank: Corporal

William A. Skrobarczyk

Branch of service: Army
Entered service: 1943
Discharge date: 1946
Places served: France
  and Belgium
Highest rank: Private
Decorations/ribbons:
  Rifleman, European
  Theater

Pedro L. Silva

Branch of service: Army
Entered service: 1944
Discharge date: 1946
Places served: Europe
Highest rank: Private
  first class
Decorations/ribbons:
  Bronze Star, Purple
  Heart, Good Conduct
  Medal, European Cam-
  paign Medal, Army of
  Occupation Medal,
  Combat Infantry Badge

David R. Slough

Branch of service:
  Air Force
Entered service: 1951
Discharge date: 1955
Places served: Korea
Highest rank: Airman
  first class

Doyle Slough

Branch of service: Navy
Entered service: 1942
Discharge date: 1946
Places served: Japan

Benjamin Dwight Spofford Sr.

Branch of service:
  Air Force
Entered service: 1918
Discharge date: 1942
Places served:
  Wright Patterson
  Air Force Base
Highest rank: Lieutenant
  colonel

S

Bill Grantford Smith

Branch of service: Marines
Entered service: 1942
Discharge date: 1946
Places served:
  South Pacific
Highest rank: Corporal
Decorations/ribbons: Rifle
  and Pistol Marksman-
  ship, Honorable Dis-
  charge Button, Service
  Lapel Button

Charles W. Stevens

Branch of service:
  Air Force
Entered service: 2000
Places served:
  Iraq and Pakistan
Highest sank: Senior
  airman

Franklin Leon Smith

Branch of service: Army
Entered service: 1944
Discharge date: 1946
Places served: Europe
Highest rank: Corporal,
  medic (surgical technician)
Decorations/ribbons:
  American Theater
  Campaign Ribbon,
  EAME Campaign Ribbon
  with one Bronze Star,
  Victory Ribbon, two
  Overseas Service Bars

Bennie Lowell Stewart

Branch of service:
  Air Force
Entered service: 1951
Discharge date: 1955
Places served: Europe,
  Texas, Washington and
  New York City
Highest rank: Sergeant
  airman first class
Decorations/ribbons:
  National Defense Medal,
  Good Conduct Medal

Louis P. Soto

Branch of service:
  Marines
Entered service: 1950
Discharge date: 1952
Places served: Korea
Highest rank: Corporal
Decorations/ribbons: Two
  Purple Heart Medals with
  Bronze Star, Korean War
  Medal, two Presidential
  Unit Citations, Korean
  Presidential Unit
  Citations, Korean War
  Service Medal

Emmett Eugene Stobbs

Branch of service: Navy
Entered service: 1941
Discharge date: 1971
Places served: South
  Pacific, Philippines,
  Korea and Vietnam
Highest rank: Lieutenant
  commander
Decorations/ribbons:
  Good Conduct Medal,
  South Pacific Medal

S

Jo Stratton

Branch of service: Navy
Places served: United States
Highest rank: Seaman

Israel Suarez

Branch of service: Army
Entered service: 1976
Discharge date: 1979
Places served: Korea

Sanders Key Stroud III

Branch of service: Army
Entered service: 1966
Killed in action: 1967
Places served: Vietnam
Highest rank: Private first class
Decorations/ribbons: Bronze Star with "V" Device, Purple Heart, Combat Infantryman's Badge

Leonard C. Suarez

Branch of service: Army
Entered service: 1955
Discharge date: 1976
Places served: Germany, Vietnam and South Pacific

Genevieve Seay Strother

Branch of service: Navy
Entered service: 1944
Discharge date: 1946
Places served: Louisiana
Highest rank: Chief yeoman

Richard C. Suarez

Branch of service: Army Air Forces
Entered service: 1942
Discharge date 1946
Places served: Aleutian Islands
Highest rank: Private first class
Decorations/ribbons: American Theater Ribbon, Asiatic-Pacific Theater Ribbon with one Bronze Battle Star, Victory Medal, Good Conduct Medal

Ernest C. 'Sleepy' Suarez

Branch of service: Navy
Entered service: 1955
Discharge date: 1963
Places served: South Pacific

Richard L. Suarez

Branch of service: Army
Entered service: 1968
Discharge date: 1971
Places served: Vietnam

Edmund Dugan Terrell
Branch of service: Navy
Entered service: 1919
Discharge date: 1921
Places served: Cavite, the Philippines and Hong Kong
Highest rank: Fireman third class

Edward O. Torres   T
Branch of service: Marines
Entered service: 1967
Discharge date: 1971
Places served: Vietnam
Highest rank: Lance corporal

Edmund Dugan Terrell Jr.
Branch of service: Army
Entered service: 1950
Discharge date: 1980
Places served: Korea, Vietnam, Cambodia, Thailand and Germany
Highest rank: Major
Decorations/ribbons: Bronze Star, Air Medal, Army Commendation Medal, Vietnam Service Medal, Army Good Conduct Medal

Eliseo M. Torres Jr.
Branch of service: Air Force
Entered service: 1974
Discharge date: 1978
Places served: Germany
Highest rank: Sergeant

Billy V. Thames
Branch of service: Air Force
Entered service: 1951
Discharge date: 1955
Places served: Texas, Florida and Kansas
Highest Rank: Staff sergeant

Rodolfo O. Torres
Branch of service: Navy and Naval Reserves
Entered service: 1971
Discharge date: Currently serving in Naval Reserves
Places served: Kuwait, Bahrain, Vietnam, Japan, Thailand, Korea and Hawaii
Highest rank: Petty officer first class

Nathaniel Thomas
Branch of service: Navy
Entered service: 1999
Discharge date: Currently serving
Places served: Texas
Highest rank: Petty officer third class

Rodolfo Ovalle Torres Jr.
Branch of service: Air Force
Entered service: 2002
Discharge date: Currently serving
Places served: Texas, Hawaii, Diego Garcia, and North Dakota
Highest rank: Staff sergeant select

T-V

Ovidio Marcos Trejo

Branch of service: Army
Entered service: 1942
Discharge date: 1945
Places served: New Guinea, Solomons and Philippines
Highest rank: Private first class
Decorations/ribbons: Five Overseas Service Bars, Asiatic-Pacific Campaign Medal with three Bronze Stars and one Bronze Arrowhead

Alberto T. Vasquez Sr.

Branch of service: Army
Entered service: 1943
Discharge date: 1946
Places served: Scotland, England, France and Belgium
Highest rank: Private first class
Decorations/ribbons: Good Conduct Medal, American Theater Campaign Medal, one Bronze Star

Floyd Herman Trudeau

Branch of service: Air Force/Army
Entered service: 1942
Discharge date: 1967
Places served: Germany, Italy, Korea and Vietnam
Highest rank: Major

Facundo Vasquez

Branch of service: Army
Places served: South Pacific

James L. Turner

Branch of service: Army
Places served: Korea
Highest rank: Second lieutenant
Decorations/ribbons: Purple Heart

Patrick D. Vasquez

Branch of service: Navy Reserves
Entered service: 1968
Discharge date: 1972
Places served: Hawaii
Highest rank: Seaman

Charles 'Chuck' Ulatoski

Branch of service: Army
Discharge sate: Currently serving
Places served: Georgia, Kentucky, Kuwait and Iraq
Highest rank: Private first class

Javier R. Venegas

Branch of service: Army
Entered service: 1967
Discharge date: 1969
Places served: Vietnam
Highest rank: Sergeant
Decorations/ribbons: Purple Heart

Feliberto G. Villa

Branch of service:
Marines
Entered service: 1965
Killed in action 1966
Places served: Vietnam

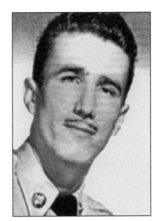

Jesus Villarreal

Branch of service: Army
Killed in action: 1951
Highest rank: Sergeant
first class
Decorations/ribbons:
Silver Star, Bronze Star

V

Gilberto Guadalupe Villanueva

Branch of service: Army
Entered service: 1986
Discharge date: 1996
Places served: Desert
Storm

Raul Romeo Villarreal

Branch of service: Army
Entered service: 1958
Discharge date: 1960
Places served:
Newfoundland and
Greenland
Highest rank: E-4

Ricardo H. Villanueva

Branch of service: Navy
Entered service: 1944
Discharge date: 1945
Places served: South
Pacific

Robert William Villarreal

Branch of service: Navy
Entered service: 1995
Discharge date: 2001
Places served: Hawaii
Highest rank:
Electrician's mate
second class

Augustin Tex Villarreal

Branch of service: Army
Entered service: 1942
Discharge date: 1943
Places served: California
Highest rank: Private
first class

Joe David Villasenor

Branch of service: Army
Entered service: 1996
Discharge date: 2002
Places served: Georgia,
Oklahoma, North Carolina
and Korea
Highest rank: Sergeant
Decorations/ribbons: Army
Commendation Medal
(three), Army Achieve-
ment Medal (six), Good
Conduct Medal (two),
Humanitarian Medal

V-W

Roberto C. Villasenor, Sr.

Branch of service: Army, Navy, Air Force and National Guard
Highest rank: Corporal
Decorations/ribbons: Vietnam Ribbon

Thomas Douglas Walters

Branch of service: Marines
Places served: Japan, Germany, Vietnam and Florida
Highest rank: Colonel

Marian French (Johnson) Wagner

Branch of service: American Red Cross
Entered service: 1948
Discharge date: 1951
Places served: Japan
Highest rank: Field director, social worker

Burl 'Doyle' Ward

Branch of service: Army
Entered service: 1944
Discharge date: 1946
Places served: Germany
Highest rank: Technician Sergeant 4
Decorations/ribbons: Bronze Star, European-African-Middle Eastern Theater Ribbon, Good Conduct Medal, World War II Victory Medal, Expert Rifle Medal

Esther C. Wall

Branch of service: Air Force
Entered service: 1958
Discharge date: 1960
Places served: New Jersey
Highest rank: Airman second class
Decorations/ribbons: Good Conduct Medal

Thomas Lee Watson

Branch of service: Navy
Entered service: 1969
Discharge date: 1973
Places served: USS Puffer and USS Guitarro

Temple Alexander Wall, Jr.

Branch of service: Navy
Entered service: 1942
Discharge date: 1954
Places served: Washington, D.C.
Highest rank: Chief
Decorations/ribbons: Navy Commendation

William Anderson Watson

Branch of service: Army
Entered service: 1943
Discharge date: 1946
Places served: Normandy and the Rhineland
Highest rank: Second lieutenant
Decorations/ribbons: Bronze Star

W

Julius William Wenzel

Branch of service: Army
Entered service: 1944
Discharge date: 1973
Places served: Germany, Korea and Vietnam
Highest rank: Sergeant major
Decorations/ribbons: Bronze Star, Purple Heart, Commendation Ribbon, Air Medal, Combat Infantry Badge

Truett Kenneth Whitmire II

Branch of service: Marines
Entered service: 1968
Discharge date: 1973
Places served: Vietnam
Highest rank: Captain
Decorations/ribbons: Distinguished Cross

Arthur M. Wharton

Branch of service: Army
Entered service: 1942
Discharge date: 1945
Highest rank: Private first class
Decorations/ribbons: Asiatic-Pacific Theater Ribbon with one Bronze Star, six Overseas Service Bars

Carlton C. Whitworth

Branch of service: Army Air Forces
Entered service: 1942
Discharge date: 1945
Places served: Europe and United States
Highest rank: Pilot

James C. Whitmire

Branch of service: Army Medical Corps
Entered service: 1970
Discharge date: 1995
Highest rank: Lieutenant colonel
Decorations/ribbons: Meritorious Service Medal, Army Commendation Medal, Army Achievement Medal, Armed Forces Reserve Medal

David A. Willis

Branch of service: Army
Entered service: 2002
Discharge date: Currently serving
Places served: Korea
Highest rank: Private

Truett Kenneth Whitmire

Branch of service: Air Force
Entered service: 1942
Places served: Germany and France
Highest rank: Major
Decorations/ribbons: Distinguished Flying Cross

Aaron D. Wille

Branch of service: Army Air Forces
Entered service: 1944
Discharge date: 1946
Places served: Europe
Highest rank: Corporal
Decorations/ribbons: Combat Infantry Badge, Bronze Star, Purple Heart, European Theater Medal with two Battle Stars, Good Conduct Medal

W-Z

Dowell Ray Williams

Branch of service: Army
Places served: Korea, Germany and Vietnam
Highest rank: Sergeant first class
Decorations/ribbons: Medal of Honor, Good Conduct Medal, Yellow Ribbon

Carlos Ybarra

Branch of service: Marines
Entered service: 1995
Discharge date: Currently serving
Places served: Japan, Iraq, Panama, Egypt and Korea
Highest rank: Captain
Decorations/ribbons: Selective Reserve, Good Conduct Medal, Overseas Service Ribbon

Tommy Charles Wimberly

Branch of service: Navy
Entered service: 1951
Discharge date: 1982
Places served: Korea, Western Pacific, Cuba, and Vietnam
Highest rank: Captain
Decorations/ribbons: Legion of Merit, Bronze Star, Meritorious Service Medal, Navy Commendation Medal, Navy Expert Pistol Medal

John A. Young

Branch of service: Navy
Entered service: 1958
Discharge date: 1961
Places served: Guam, Japan, China, South Pacific and California
Highest rank: Seaman
Decorations/ribbons: China Service

Ernest M. Wood

Branch of service: Air Force
Entered service: 1953
Retired date: 1973
Places served: Bermuda, Thailand, Florida, Washington, Oklahoma, Colorado, Ohio and Washington, D.C.
Highest rank: Major

Alfredo V. Zamora

Branch of service: Army
Entered service: 1963
Places served: Germany

William Newhall Worley

Branch of service: Navy
Entered service: 1990
Discharge date: Currently serving
Places served: Cuba, New York, New Jersey, California
Highest Rank: Petty officer second class

Salvador M. Zuniga

Branch of service: Army
Entered service: 1993
Places served: Fort Hood, California and Washington
Highest rank: First lieutenant
Decorations/ribbons: Army Commendation Medal, Army Achievement Medal, National Defense Service Medal

South Texas Heroes

A CELEBRATION OF OUR MILITARY

Project staff

Linda Montoya, project manager

Fernando Ortiz Jr., editor and designer

James Simmons, cover designer and photographer

Frank Lemos, Letty Hinojosa, Steve Stewart, Mari Stone
and **Richard Vela Garcia,** project imagers

Additional thanks to the following people who contributed photos or otherwise helped with this book:
Steve Arnold, Lisette Banda, Jason Crane, Sandra Garza, Murphy Givens, Vilma Jimenez, Jennifer Kelley,
Kevin Kerrigan, Tom Kreneck (Texas A&M University-Corpus Christi), Cindy Munoz, Christina Montoya,
Mari-Ann Montoya, Margaret Neu, Melisa Padilla, Mary Beth Smith, and Jorge Vidrio.

Corpus Christi Caller-Times

An E.W. Scripps Company

Larry L. Rose, Publisher

Libby Averyt, Editor

Contributors of cover images

FRONT COVER (from left):
Denise and **Juan M. Garcia III**
Dress uniform cap: **Luther G. Jones, Jr.**
Pablo Padilla
Dogtags: **Claude V. D'Unger**
Pilot and medal: **Lloyd (Pete) Hughes**

BACK COVER (from left):
Robert E. McCullough
Richard Michael Rodriguez
Medals: **Floyd Herman Trudeau**
Clarice B. Jones

FRAMED OVAL PORTRAIT ON PAGE 1:
Fred. O. Garza

We thank all contributors for trusting us with their treasures.